Introduction

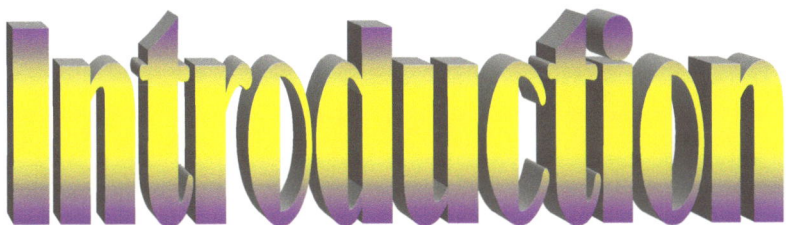

As an artist of any kind they are struggles you are going to have to face. The first thing I ever wanted to be was an artist like Monet and Picasso. My mother told at the age of four years old that I shouldn't be an artist because they don't make any money. Quickly, that made me change my mind and I wanted to be a doctor for a while. I have been through different phases, but always found my way back to art.

There was only so long that I could deny the fact that I am meant to be an artist. It took some time for my mother to become supportive of me pursuing a career as an artist, but eventually she came around. My mother said that she tried to stop me from becoming an artist because she didn't want me to struggle, and now she says, "If struggling makes you happy then I'm happy for you."

The reason I wanted to reach out to other artists and get their own story was because we don't always have a support system to lean on to. This project is meant to be raw and unpolished with each individual artist using their own voice. The art and entertainment world is a difficult world to break into and survive in. Knowing that there are other artists that feel the same way, and have felt like giving up at times can give us all hope.

Sometimes all it takes is someone to give you just a chance. Inspiration can come from many places. Opportunities come and go, and it's hard not to get discourage when you don't get what you want. Someone that has inspired me, and has kept me going came from an unexpected place. One day I was listening to Tyra Banks reminisce about her old modeling days. She said in one day she went to seven or eight modeling agencies, and they all rejected her except that last one of the day said yes to her. You have to respect someone for having that kind of drive to not give up. So whenever I don't get my way I feel sorry for myself for a minute, and then move on because there is so much else out there.

I don't want any artist to give up on their dreams if that is what they are truly passionate about, even if that means that there is going to be more competition for me. Just listening to different artists can put things in perspective, and hopefully open minds to the possibilities we can achieve.

-Sarah Ghanooni

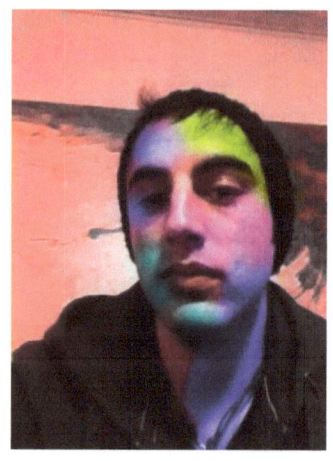

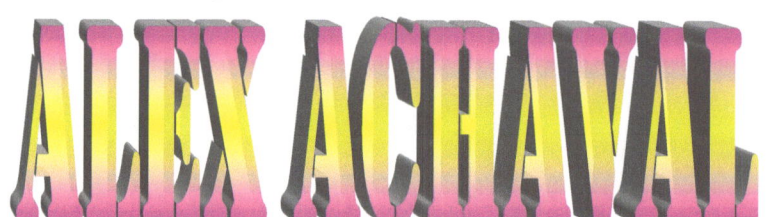

Born on October 16th 1986 and grew up in a tiny town in the middle of Washington state called Ellensburg. I always loved to draw when I was younger and was good at it, but definitely not a little prodigy. It wasn't until high school when I began to get serious about drawing and painting. I always loved black and white drawings and never wanted to paint like a stubborn little kid stuck in his ways about hating broccoli he has not tried. When I did try it my opinion totally flipped and after high school I really started eating a lot of broccoli.

Musicians and Icons inspired a lot of my early work, doing a lot of portraits of all the stereotypical people painted, such as Monroe, Dean, Marley, and so on, but also inspired by Dali with a surreal twist. I really have a hard time determining what kind of painting I really do now because my painting is so diverse and love painting in all different styles, mediums, and subjects. I take my inspiration these days from how I'm feeling at that moment or that time in my life, painting a lot of emotion into my work. If I am sad then a sad man I shall paint, If something just catches my interest, I'll incorporate something I've felt in my life with that subject. For example in my painting "Letting Go" I took the feeling and emotion of heartache and loss in the face and body with bees escaping the head representing the person leaving your mind. It lets you interpret the painting in your own way and relate to it.

I am also very inspired by pop art and taking simple subjects like hotdogs that no one would look at as a piece of art and turning it into a piece that works such as Warhol did with various pieces. Also I am simply inspired by almost every other artist in this world. When I go to an art show or see good and meaningful art I'm so amazed and taken back by everyone's work that it pushes me to take my painting to another level as soon as possible.

I am a painter because it's an escape. It's a way to unravel. It's a way to express myself just as a musician writes a song and an author writes a book, I write a painting. Just like authors and writers we get painters block. It's a struggle to be an artist and to get yourself out there and known. It's a struggle to get something popular, make someone want something without other people wanting it as well. When it comes down to it the hardest part of all of it is the painting in itself. The dedication it takes to gain a collection of work, coming up with a niche and style that is all your own is challenging and it takes a lot of blank canvas, brainstorming, creativity, research and time. But in time your style will find you. I got simple and great advice from someone who said "Just paint or sketch every single day no matter what."

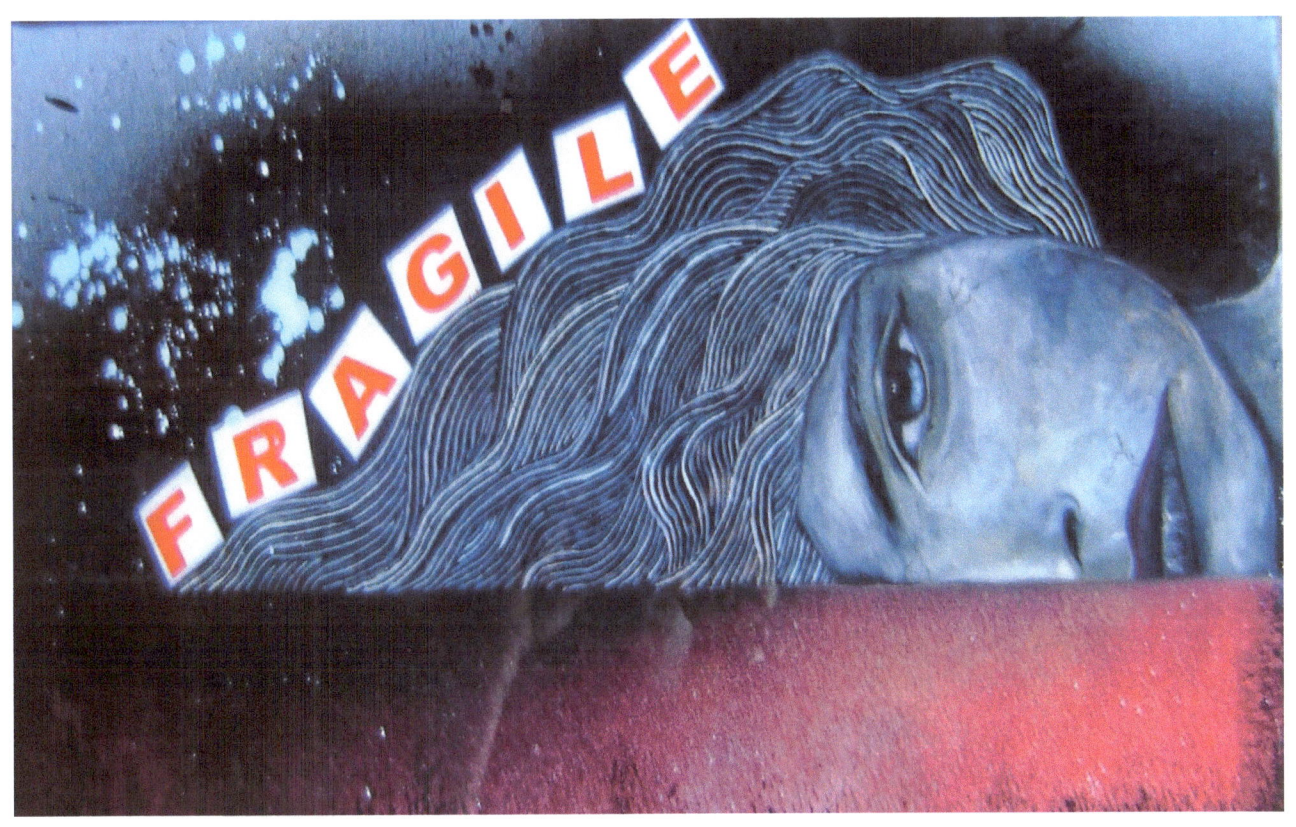

"Fragile" Alex Achavel , mixed media 2010

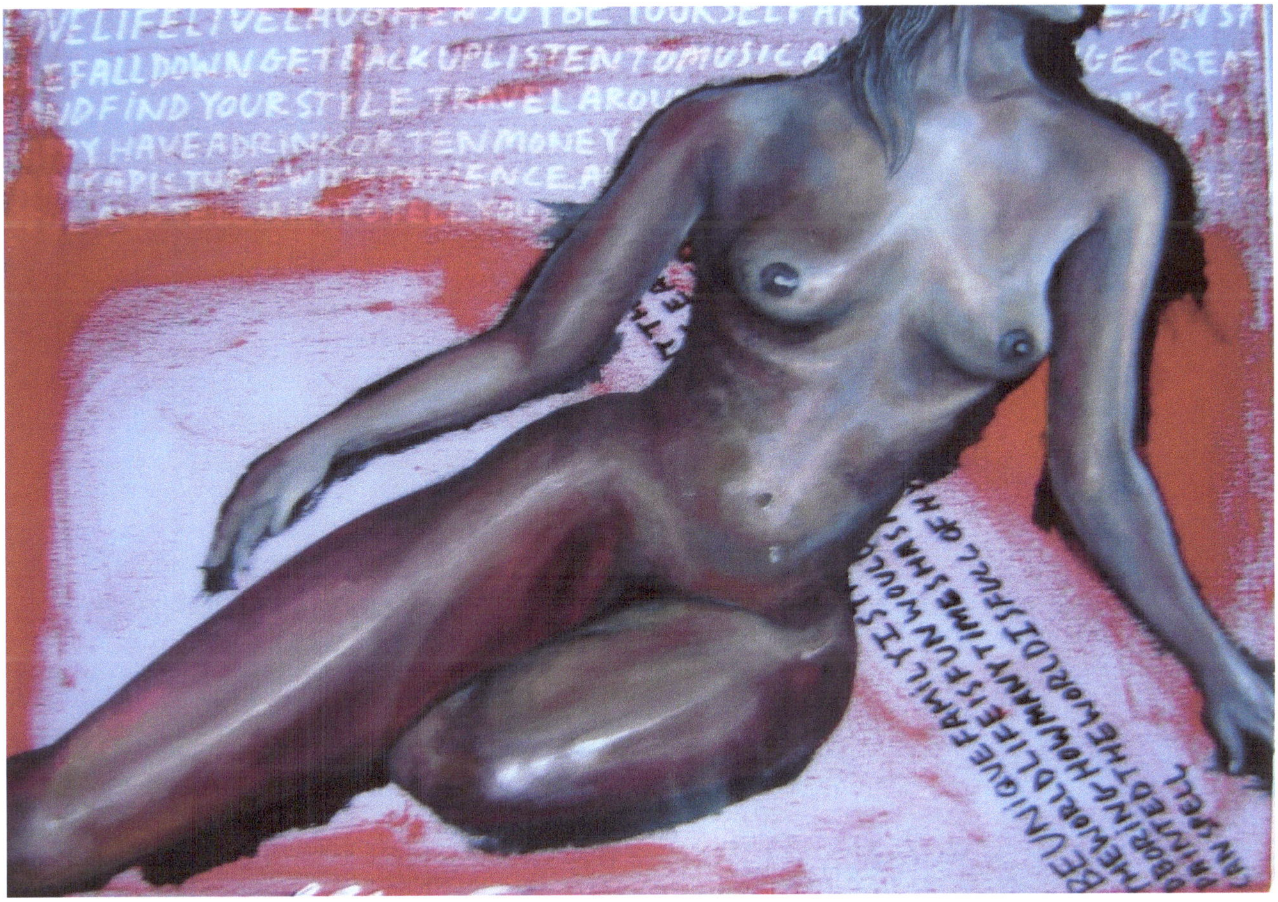

"Whoever you are" Alex Achavel, mixed media 2010

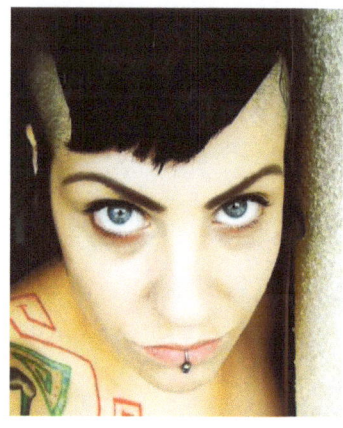 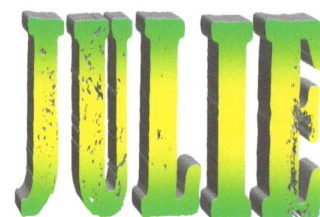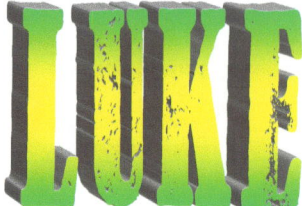

I started painting when I was a child; like many children do to appease self fulfillment of experimentation and curiosity. But as I grew, watched and learned, I started to realize what the world truly was for me, and my art became a way of life to cope with living in the dark and wanting to be in the light.

This world seen through my child eyes was adversity, confusion and a life of struggle. The only beauty and true happiness of comfort and safety came through this new world I cherished in artwork, Here i could be anyone and see anything I desired it to be.

Art to me is that parent that was never there, that friend who never went away, that world that never failed me. My love for art, indeed without exaggeration saved my life.

This is very important to who i am as an artist, and for others to understand what art means to me and what my work is about. I am an artist of the subconscious, I feel my body is the vessel to bring out these works, and the product of where I was in my mind and soul at that moment, my art is my story. I can control Lucidity through my work, it's a trance like state where nothing around me is present just that moment in time and nothing can touch me. These moments of mental bliss have helped me fight my way out of adversity.

My body of work is never completely cohesive due to the constant movement of life around me. Life and living is my muse, life is my art degree. I navigate by my rules, simply because I can, and I refuse to lose what art has been for me in the past and what it will continue to be for my future. The only thing in my life I have never compromised with is my art.

My advice for other artists is stay true to who you are no matter what, just believe in yourself and what makes you happy regardless of what other artists or people in society are creating or what's popular at that moment. I have come across many people who either love or hate what I do, but that's alright it's still an emotion that is being roused in them, grasp tightly what makes your art important to you that is where your work will be true and it will shine.

I believe when people view my work it's not necessarily the imagery they are attracted to completely, but it's that moment of real passion for the love of creating that I put into ever piece that makes it more than the image they love, or hate. Be real, give the world your gift, and never say sorry for doing so.

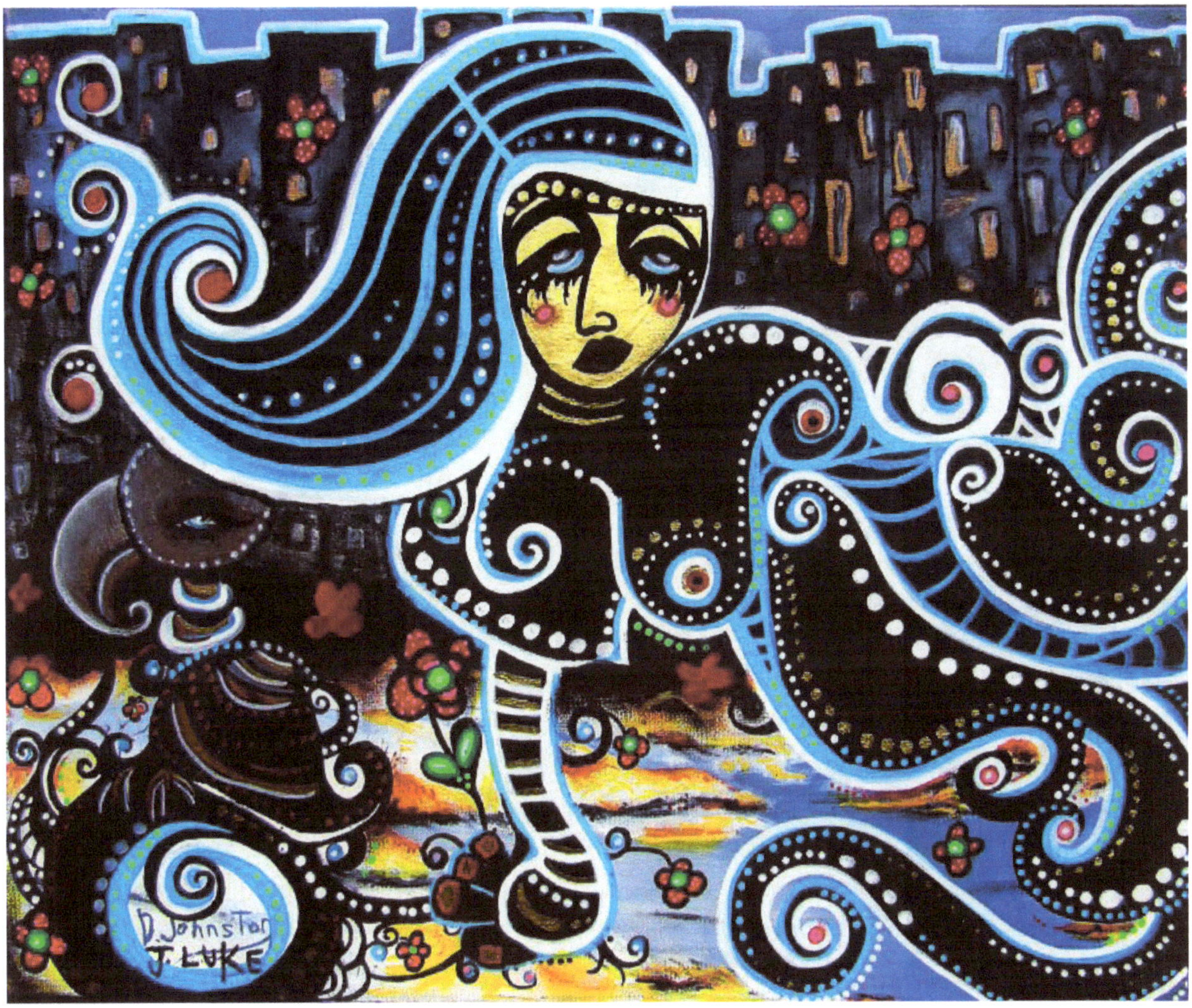

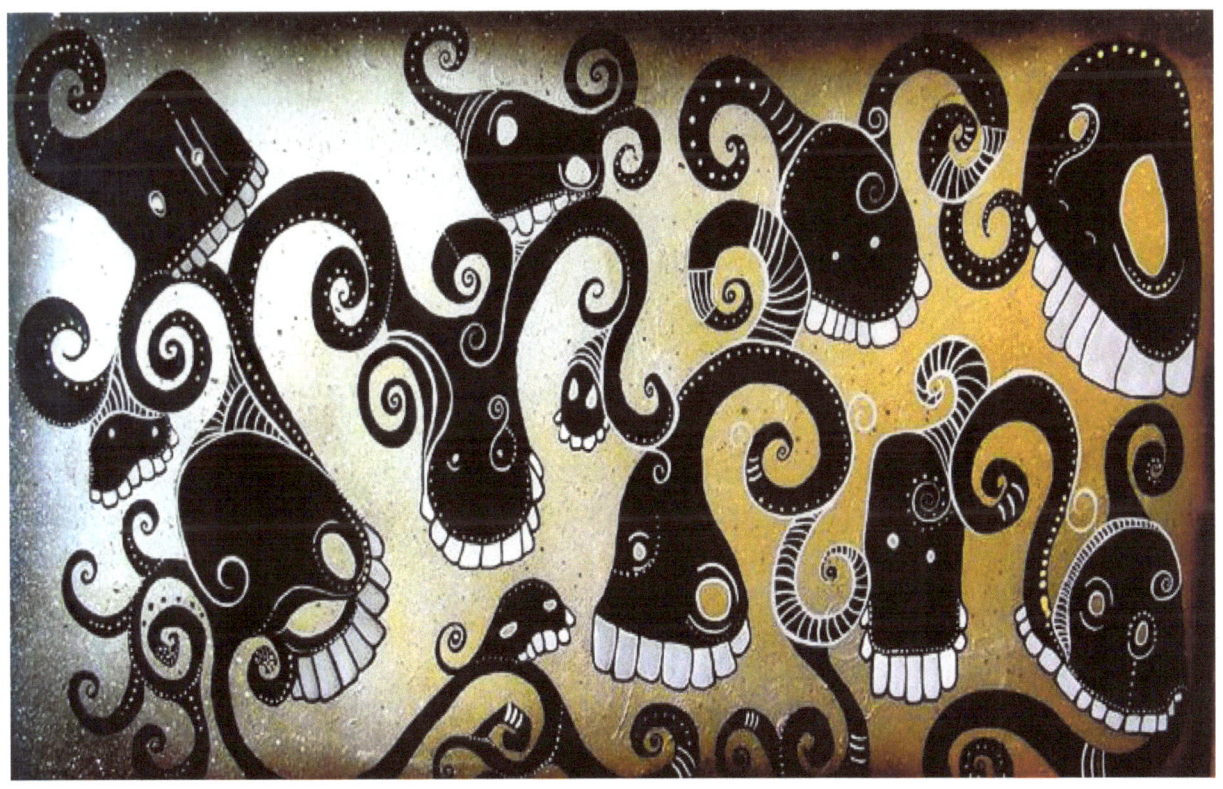

"Piece of You" Julie Luke (collaborative with D. Johnston) 2009 16x20 oil & acrylic on canvas

"Family of Ula" Julie Luke, 24x36 acrylic on canvas 2007

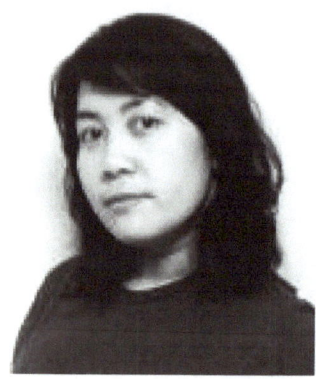

Banchong Douangphrachanh

Clothing is valuable. It's one of the essentials, just behind food and shelter. Clothes protect us from the elements. They give us protection when we interact with our environment. I value the ability of clothes to extend our boundary and push nature. People who push the limits to go higher, harder, and faster inspire me. I believe I can make the type of clothing that can propel people to push the limit of what they can do.

Alongside super performance, I strive to make clothes with great care, craftsmanship, and longevity. Days of mass production and cheap imitation won't be gone any time soon, but the next generation of designers will be pushing quality and wear-ability to new level. I want my clothing to have its own story that people talk about- to build its own legend.

People always asked me, "Where do you get your inspiration?" Was it a painting, architecture, or perhaps nature?

Yes, yes and yes to all of these answers. Inspiration comes from everywhere. It takes form in literal images or it can be conceptual; this is one of my favorite aspects of designing. For instance, I like geometry and mathematical equations. I will analyze and dissect the problem and then translate that to my design. Philosophy is also another good inspiration. I'll do background research on a particular idea of a philosopher and once I understand the concept, I'll apply that idea to my design. Double-helix DNA molecules, cross-section machining parts, fingerprints- there's so much great inspiration to be had!

I was born in Laos shortly after the communist took over. My father was an intellectual under the previous government and therefore in danger under the communists. When I was six, my family escaped across the Mekong River (which separates Laos from Thailand) late at night with as much jewelry as we could take. Our family spent several weeks in jail, a year in a Thai Refugee camp, and most of our jewelry in bribes before we could secure sponsorship to America.

Clearly, I wasn't born into an artistic family. As a Laos child, I never knew anyone who could draw, paint, or create sculpture. I hadn't heard of drawing classes until I came to America. So to learn what I needed for my craft, I had to get educated. Three years, loads of debt, and a Masters of Fine Art Fashion Design degree later, I was injected with a heavy dose of skills ready to make at dent in the world.

When I see my work on the national scene, I am amazed by the impossibility of the event. A refugee from a poor third world country emerging out of the shadows; the statistics against it seem insurmountable.

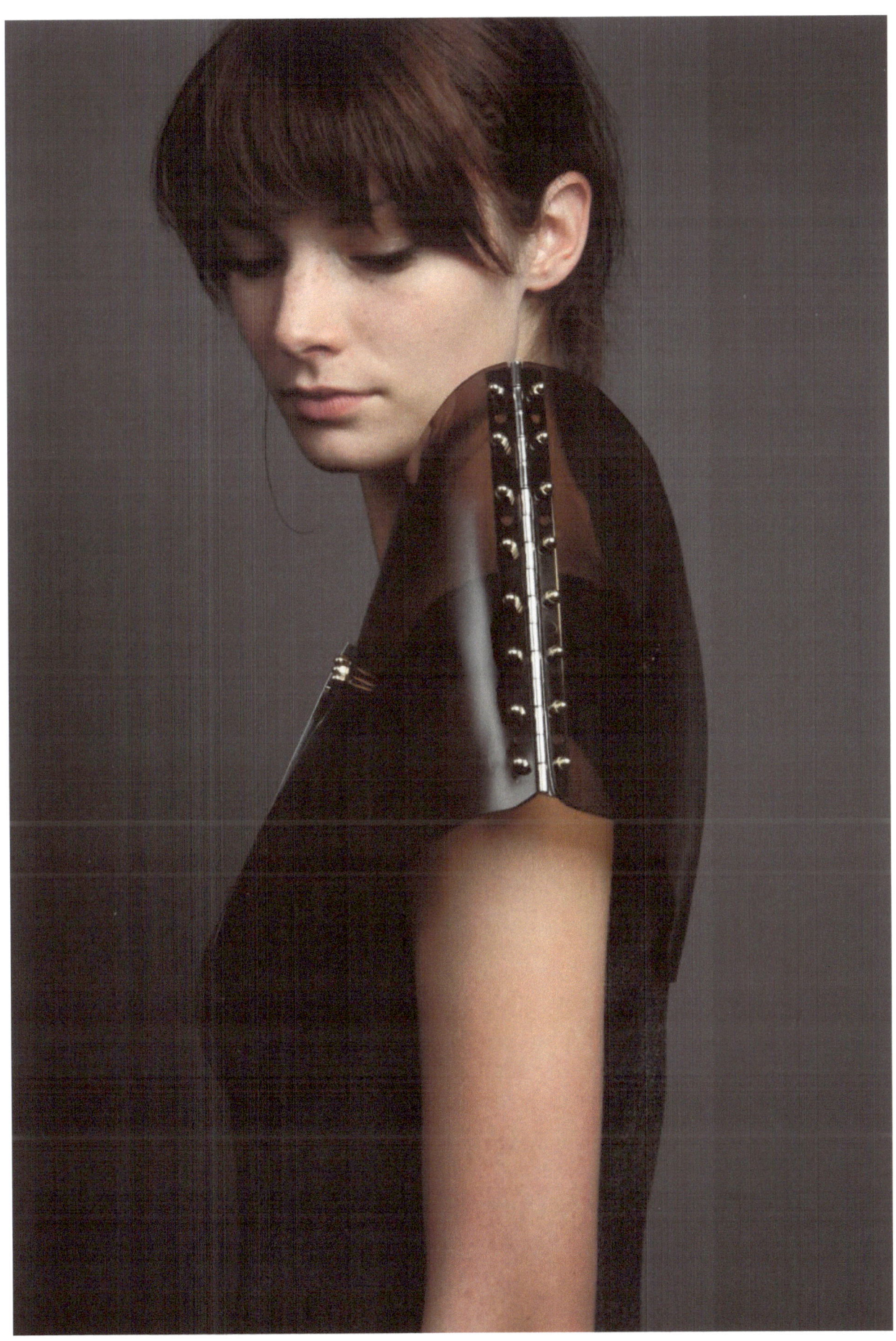

"Acrylic top with rivets and clamps." Banchong Douangphrachanh , Wool Dress. 2008

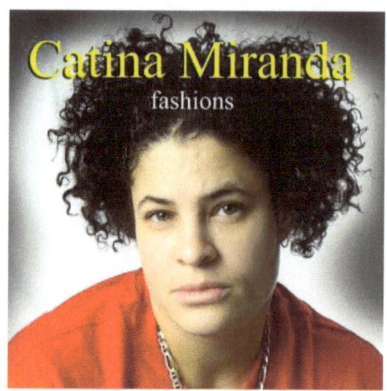

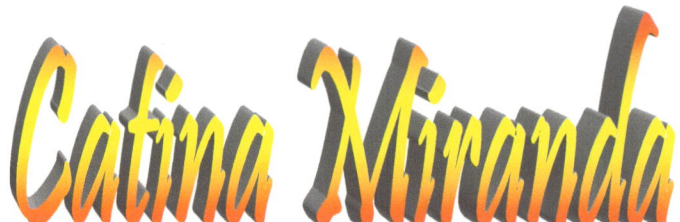

I'd like to thank GOD for keeping me focused. I use to not like my name until I got older when I found out what it meant. Catina means pure and Miranda means strange and wonderful. Only time will tell if I can live up to such a great name for an artist. I was born on August 16th 1972 in Newark, New Jersey .We moved back to Williamsburg Va. were I was raised. My mom said I just got up and started walking as a baby, I guess that's why I crawl so much now. I started expressing myself early with art and it helped me cope with being molested at seven by the children in my neighborhood. That's why I think my style is childlike surrealism.

I got trapped in the past or something like that...

I wrote the book called The Battle within 1972 –2012 about my crazy childhood. The key to peace John 14:27

Inside the house was where love was the battlefield.

My parents were too young to have us.

My art style that I mentioned earlier is what I call childlike surrealism. I do logos to murals as well as draw from my dreams and nightmares. Those that inspire me are GOD, Salvador Dali, my mother, and my father. He has the love to paint landscapes; I think that's where I got my talent and love for it as well. His inspiration is Bob Ross. My mom is real creative too in design and decorating.

My advice to other artists is to never sell your soul. Do what I did; paint your soul for everyone to see and hopefully understand the power of your expression. And never ever give up on your dreams. I always pray just to make it through every day; it's a struggle out there, especially for artists today. I had a hard life growing up, but because of those very same hardships I am able to turn my mess into a message for others.

First I'd like to thank Sarah an angel for this great opportunity and the experience to develop as an artist on worldwide scale and for allowing me to enter her world and then a special thanks to Ms. Maria Thorton for listening to me at 3am when needed someone to talk too. Finally thanks to James T. Overton

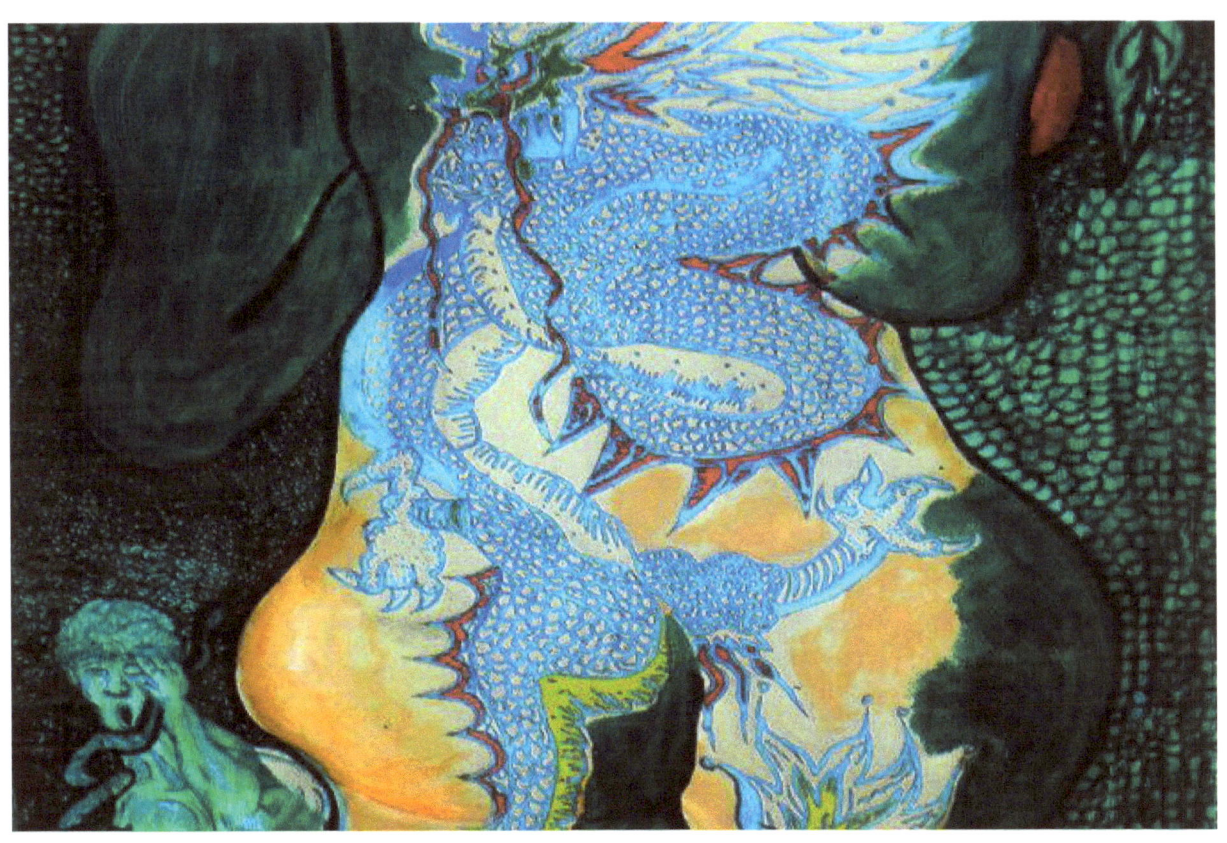

"Eve Project" Catina Miranda

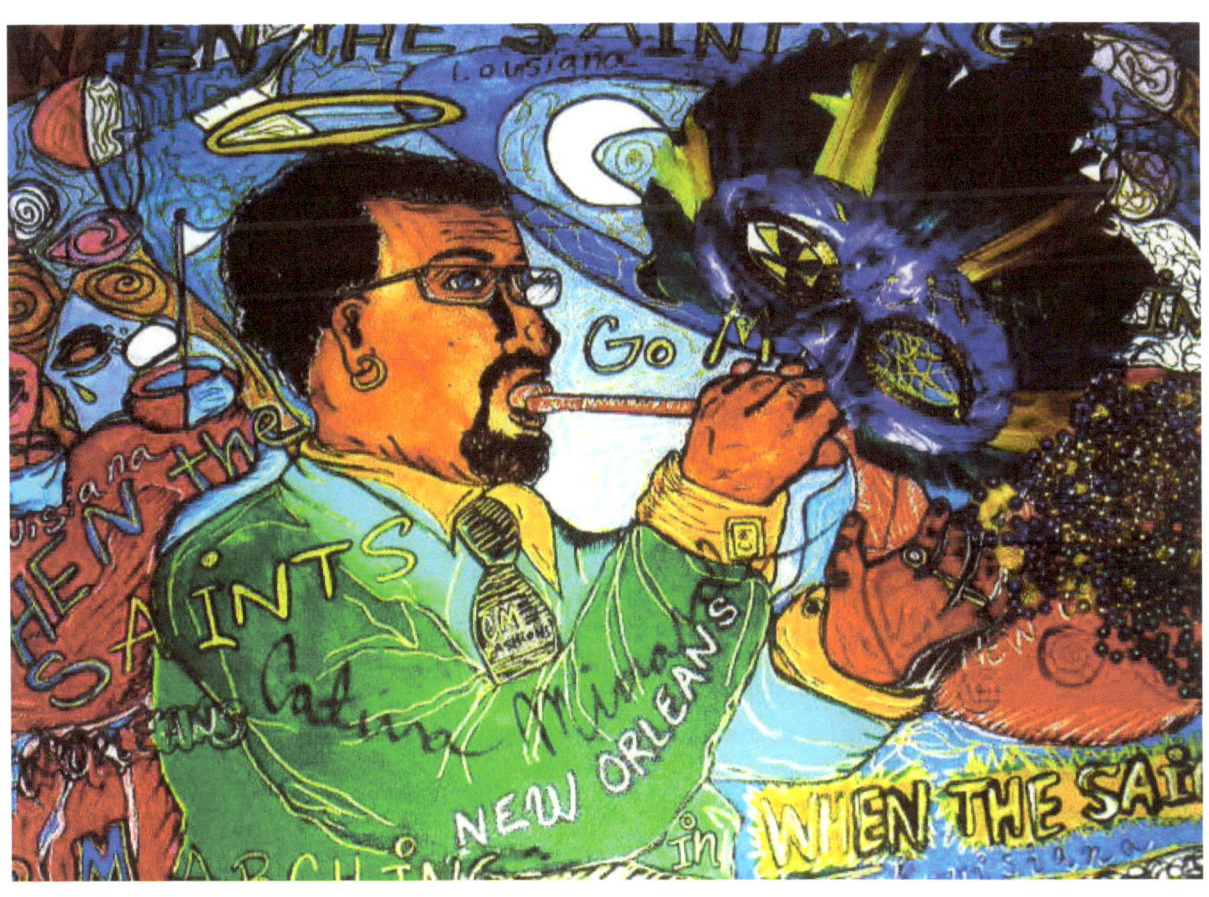

"Go Saints!" Catina Miranda

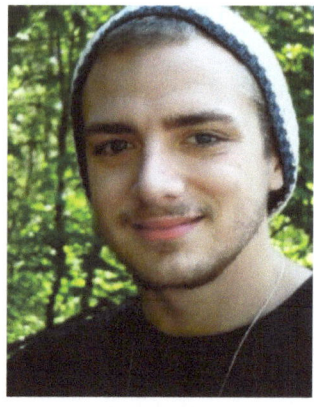

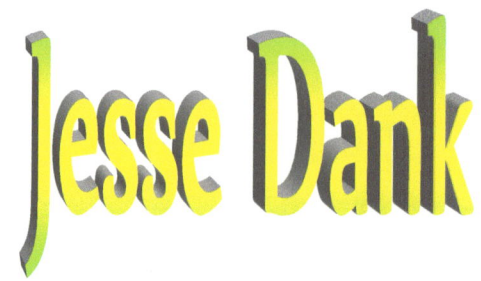

My name is Jesse Dank. I'm 19, I was born in 1990. I paint the special "wet on wet" oil technique. I was raised in the slums and thought to be street smart. I was introduced into crime and narcotics at a young age. I always had a love for mother- nature but didn't know how that would play into my life. I just assumed, like everyone else in my family I would be an outlaw and end up in prison or dead.. That's just how life was.

Every day after school my friends and I would go home, blaze and watch Bob Ross. We loved it. We loved how he worked "inside" the canvas. He would take you on a trip that was always calm and suspenseful. We knew that nothing could make that man angry, and we wanted that peace of mind. We watched Bob Ross everyday for years.

One day I decided I was going to try and paint. I loved nature and Bob said I could. I bought some cheap paint and got on it. To my surprise I was good. I've never taken a class or lessons but I was decent. At that moment I knew I was going to paint for the rest of my life.

As I got better I realized that this is what I wanted to do with my life. I wanted to be an artist that was real to life. I started selling paintings on eBay and festivals. I don't make much, but the more art I get out, the better.

Painting has done something unreal in my life. I used to be on a lot of drugs and getting into trouble, but painting has replaced that completely. I had severe paranoia, but in that canvas I don't feel that way. It's my world; there is no unpleasant vibes there. Painting takes paranoia completely away. It has changed my life in a way I can't describe, it's just beautiful.

I take a lot of pride in Washington State. The nature is beautiful, the vibe is unreal. I always take the side of the struggling man. Their life is hard, I was there. To this day my father is homeless and my mother an addict. No matter how I change, I will always be kicking on a corner with my family dealing with their struggles. You can't turn your backs on the ones that need you.

I want to find away to bring the power of painting to them, the struggling people. Even if it's just looking at a piece of art to escape the oppression or paranoia. I paint for the struggling man. They inspire me. I meet people and feel their struggle. So in turn I go home and paint for them. I'll paint a place where they can feel at home, with no worries or frustrations. Painting can save lives, it saved mine.

I sell paintings cheap because everyone should be able to own something as powerful as a piece of art. Every year I'm at Seattle Hempfest giving art to people who are in need of it. I will always have love for people and art.

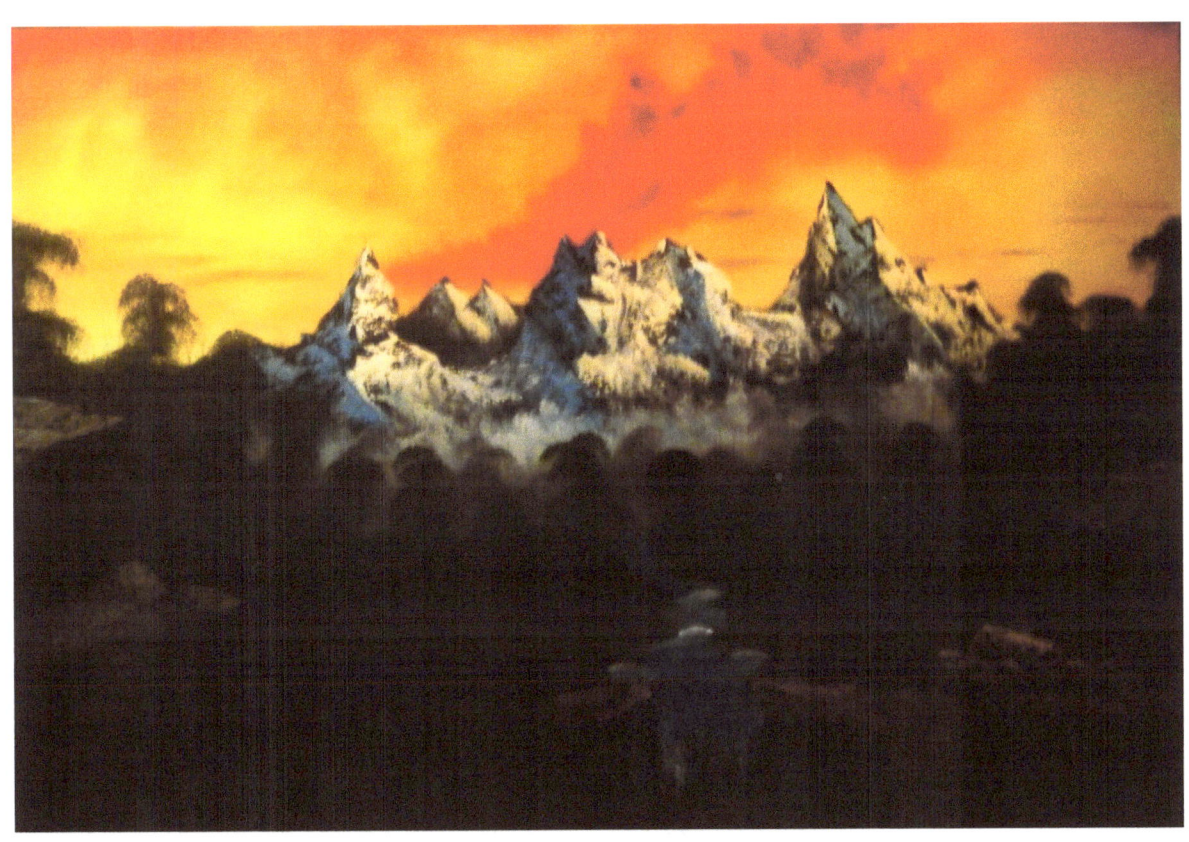

"Prehistoric Earth" Jesse Dank, done in oil paint. Dimensions 24" by 36". 2009

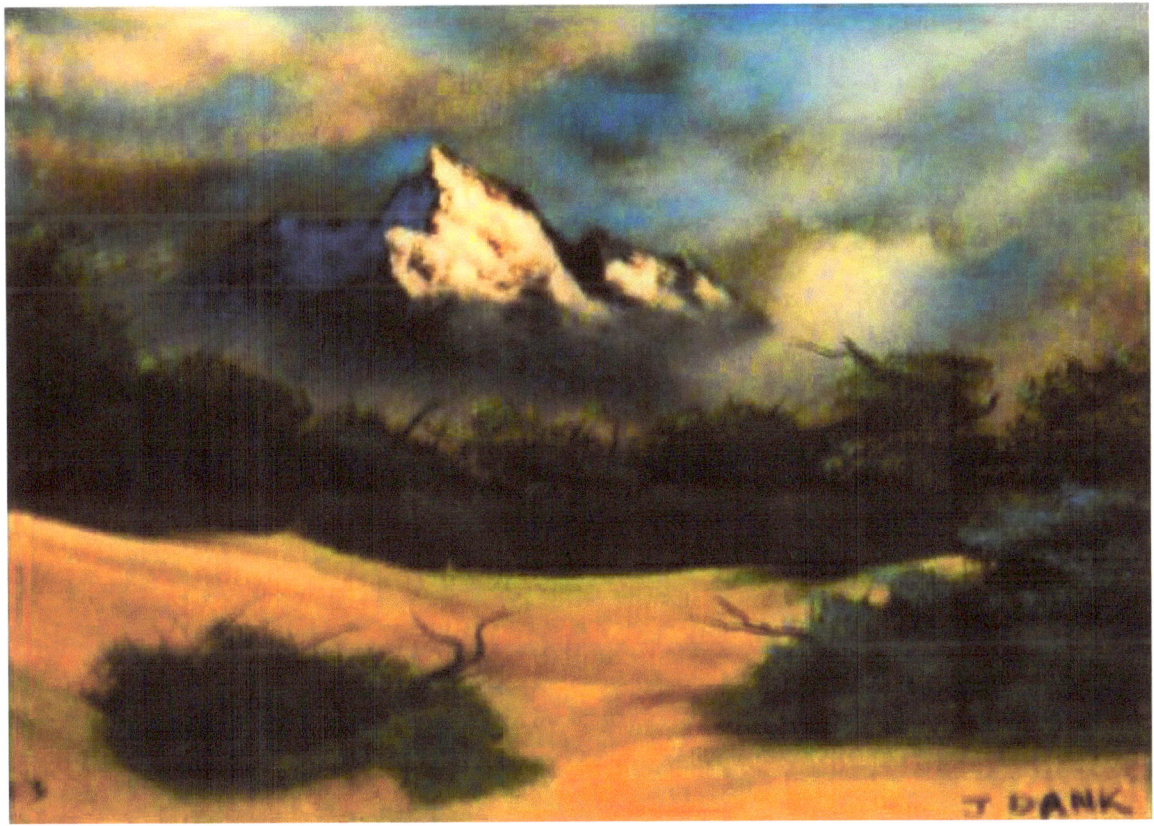

"Seascape" Jesse Dank. done in oils, 16" by 20". 2009

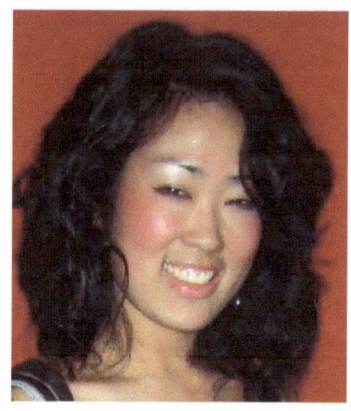

Tanya Min Jee

To dream, to do, and to trust yourself are words I live by daily. I am a fashion designer but first and foremost I am an artist: highly intuitive, emotionally driven, passionate, a lover of process, and a need to create. I thank my family who acknowledged my passion for the arts at a young age and created an artistically enriching environment where I was free to observe, question, analyze, and experiment to the fullest.

My father, a skilled artisan who dabbled in many fine art mediums before settling into a career in architecture, was the first family member to introduce me into the world of fine art and craft. Everyday seemed to be "fathers-take-your-daughter-to-work-day". I would watch in awe as he discussed business with prospective clients, work hard on the job site, and see the end result: an aesthetically beautiful, well-constructed home and more importantly a satisfied client. He embodied everything I wanted to be as a designer, craftsman and person: full of passion, talent, integrity and genuine charisma.

The first fine art medium I explored was charcoal drawing. I remember going through my older sister's fashion magazines and compiling tears of fashion models and being particularly interested to draw their faces. I would run up to my father, eager to show him my latest creation only to receive feedback reminiscent to "sweetie, this is nice but the eyes are a little too far apart, the nose is not proportional to the face, and the shading is a bit too rough." It was his long winded response of saying my drawing was just "ok". I did not want "ok"--in fact I hated the word "ok". I wanted so badly to improve. He taught, I actively listened, and I practiced diligently. One drawing every month turned into one drawing a week to one drawing a day. I will never forget the day I showed my father a drawing of supermodel Kate Moss. He stopped and stared at the charcoal portrait with a sparkle in his eye. I call this "sparkle" a moment of paternal pride and it was my turning point as an artist. Its experiences like this that made me realize the importance of passion, discipline, repetition, and patience: these qualities changed my work and brought it ultimately to a new level.

I kept drawing in my younger years which somehow organically drifted towards fashion. While clipping out magazine tears of models, I started to pay attention to the clothing and began identifying trends, designer labels, figure flattering silhouettes, and fabrics that spoke to me. My sense of style evolved quickly and found myself taking risks in my middle school and high school years coordinating unusual color combinations, wearing plaids with prints and such. My personal style was distinct and surprisingly well received among my fellow classmates.

So here I am today living the dream I envisioned since I was twelve years old. In the year and a half I have been designing I have been blessed with beautiful opportunities and overwhelming recognition. What is my secret? Aside from incredible mentors who always "led by example" like my father and a fierce discipline to never stop learning, practicing, and perfecting? Here are my top 3 life lessons:

1 | Keep your eye on the prize: the road to success has a lot of ups and downs supplemented with moments / people that can inspire doubt. Do not distract yourself from the prize. Learn and grow from every good and bad experience; cherish those that enrich your life and let go of those that don't.

2 | Hone your craft: let your work speak volumes about you as an artist / person.

3 | Stay humble. Arrogance impedes on any improvement on craft and character.

And always remember, never stop dreaming, doing, and believing in yourself.

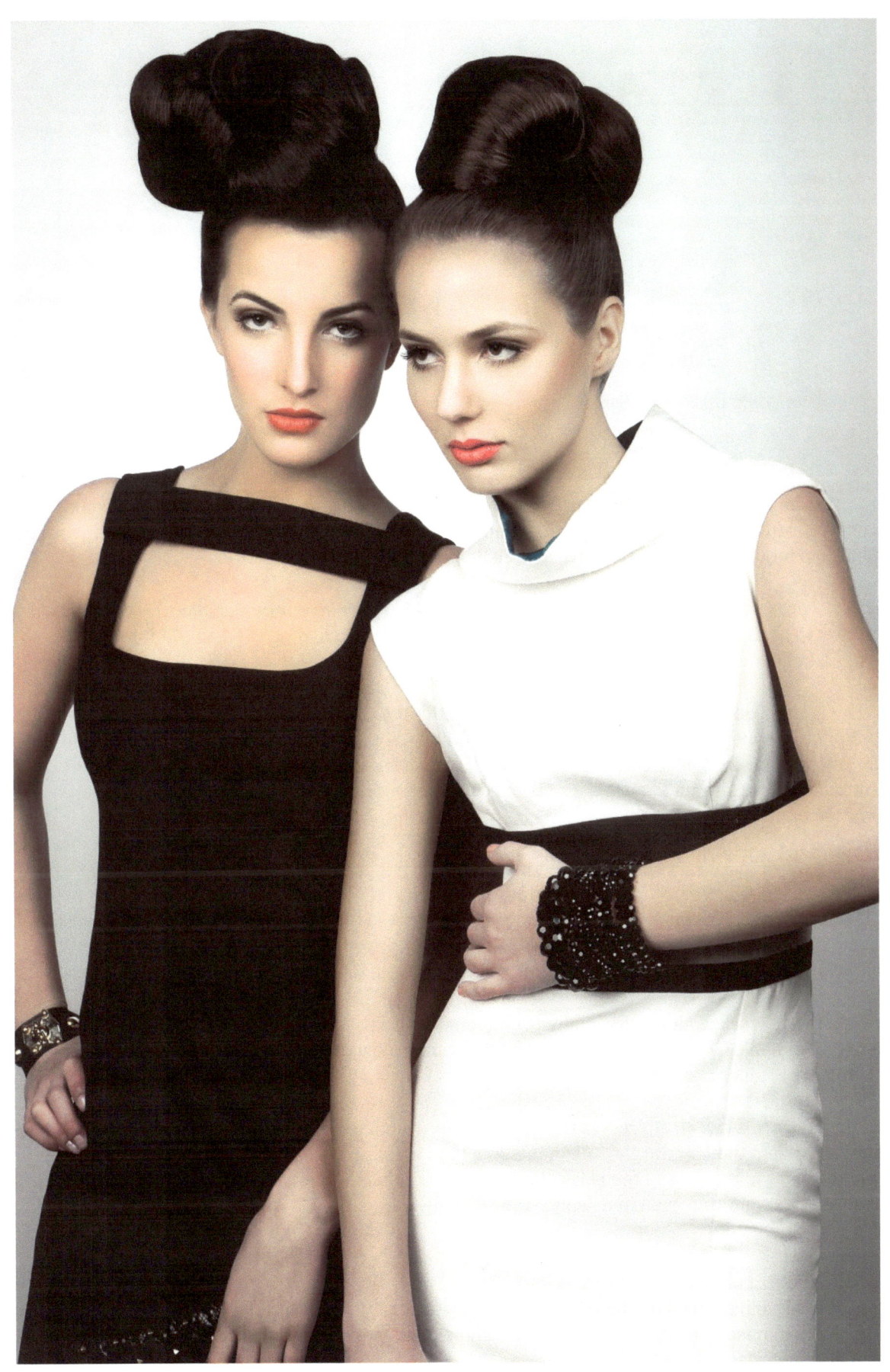

Tanya Min Jee designs (photo by Peter Gaan)

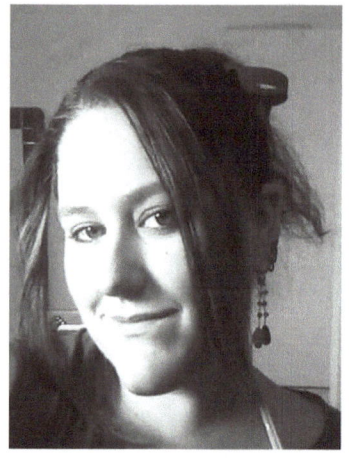

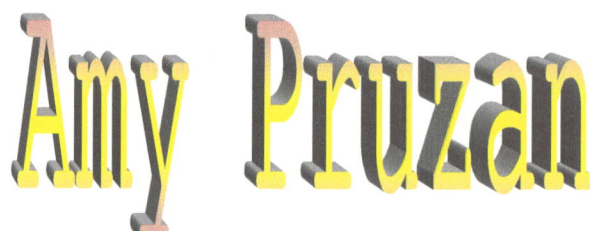

Memories are liquid. They are rain drops, fragmented snapshots of history. Over time memories can fade and sharpen, metamorphose, or completely dissolve. I am interested in memory, as both an intimate personal treasure as well as a tangible historical record.

I am intrigued by the way people seem to be able to reinvent their memories to favor what could have been, or forget tragedies that should never have occurred. What might it feel like to suffer from Alzheimer's and lose the memories of your life?

Lewis Hine, once said, "Photographs tell the truth…but photographers lie." To me this means that for a photographic image to exist, something in it had to be real. To be able to physically hold a photograph is to freeze time, to capture and preserve a moment. However even photographs can be manipulated and altered to an artist's vision. So, in my mind photographs and memories share many common bonds.

I work in a variety of media, but maintain a strong focus on glass, metal and photography. I earned her B.F.A degree, Magna Cum Laude, from Cornish College of the Arts in 2006, with triple majors in sculpture, print, and photography. I have studied at institutions such as Alexander Muss in Israel, Pilchuck Glass School, and Pratt Fine Arts Center. I work resides in several permanent collections including the Fred Hutchinson Cancer Research Center.

I have worked along-side many prominent local artists, such as Sonja Blomdahl, Ginny Ruffner, and Martin Blank. I was honored with both the Corning award nomination form Pilchuck Glass School, and the Art Bridge Scholarship from Pratt Fine Arts Center.

My current work addresses the questions of what happens to our memories over the passage of time. I like to think of the glass elements as a type of lens to contain my memories. As images float from the front to the back of the glass, they can either come in to focus or be distorted. Glass as a material is a liquid, and even in its solid state, it is always changing. And that physical property heavily influences my work.

I view photographic images as both a literal and metaphoric representation of memory. I'm also interested in environmental memory, or the relationship between nature and the civilizations of man. By juxtaposing the metal structures, with the photographic memories, I challenge viewers to consider their place in the world.

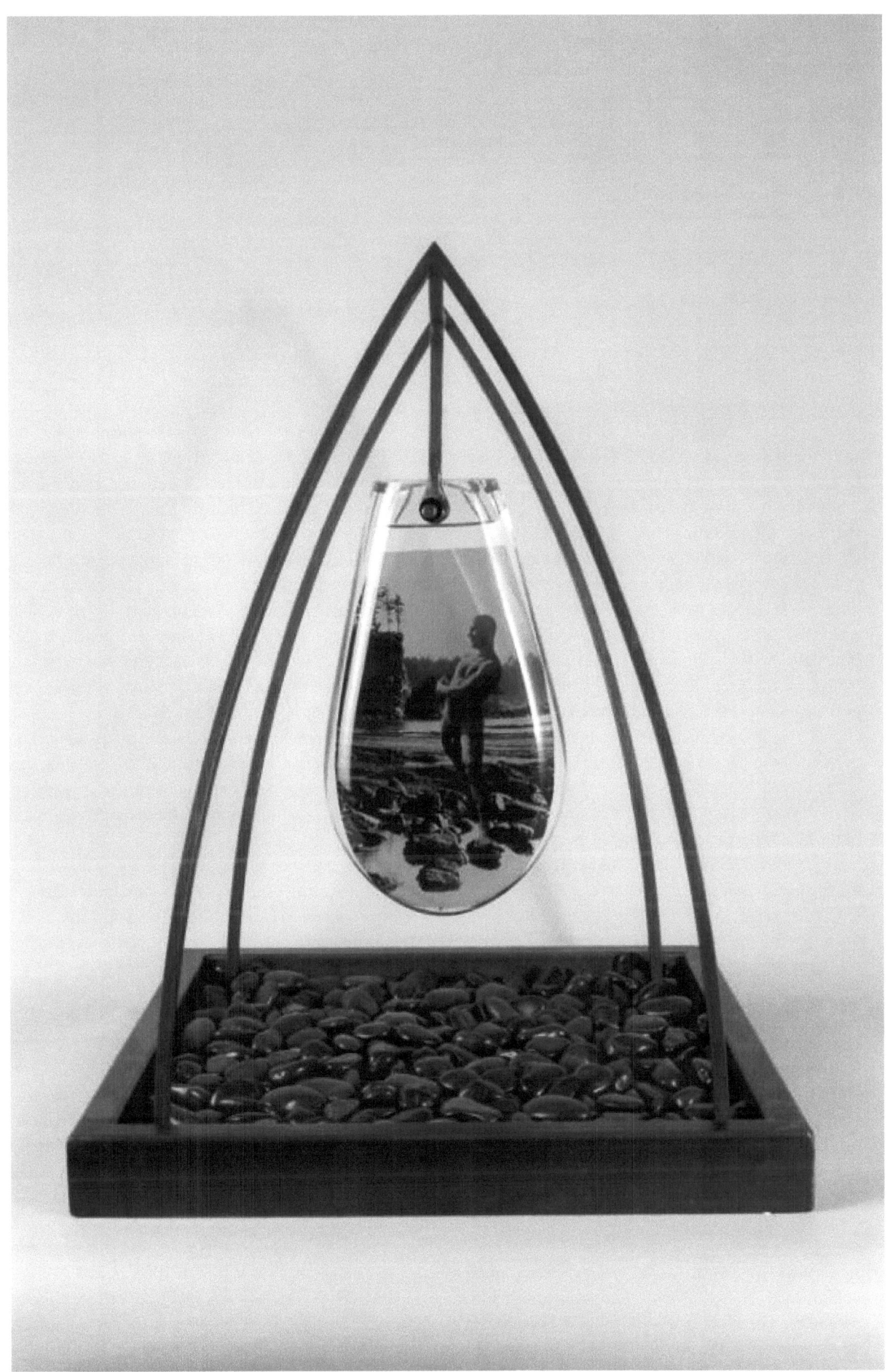

Amy Pruzan

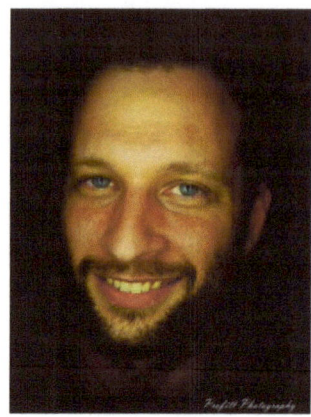

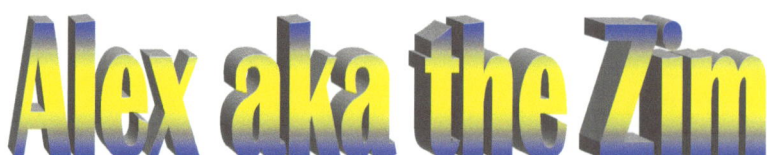

I love music, music is my passion. There is hardly a time when I am not listening, playing, or thinking about music. I love being effected by music; I love to feel bass in my chest, or have well sang harmonies vibrate the back of my head, or hear the sweet thick tone of a well played guitar. I love it when music sparks a memory. In the winter of 1999 I intentionally bought and exclusively listened to Fiona Apple's "When the Pawn" album while I spent a week in New York City. To this day when I play that album I am brought back to my experience there, specifically riding on the subway. I spent a lot of time on the subway.

While I was in New York I also realized I did not like to be alone. I was alone most of my time there. Over the years music has been one of my best companions. Whatever emotion I am experiencing music is there with me, to help me cope, celebrate, calm me, or get me pumped. I feel fortunate that I not only get to listen to music but I also get to create it. I started playing music in fourth grade at Our Lady of Fatima in Seattle, Washington. My parents rented me an Alto Saxophone. I still remember the first day I got it I put it together from my memory of seeing it done at school. I did it almost right; I had the mouth piece on upside down. I sat outside on our front lawn and honked away.

My first performance as a musician was on my front lawn. From that day on I have been playing and performing music. It wasn't till my sophomore year at Franklin high school that the musical bug really bit down hard. I watched and listened to the Jazz band at the end of the year concert, and I was hooked. Not so much for what they were playing but more for how they affected the audience. I wanted to be a part of that conversation; to be on stage creating and receive the audience's response to it.

 I went to Shoreline Community College focused on music, took theory and played in the Jazz band, among other bands. I got my Associates Arts degree and transferred to the University of Washington. Here is where my aspirations came to a screeching halt. The UW music school and I did not mix. It was painful, I could not take it anymore after two quarters I had enough and walked out the front door. In front of me was the UW school of art, I always had an aptitude for art.

I just wanted to be on stage performing, and would do whatever I needed to accomplish that. So when Kevin Sawka, the best drummer I ever played with, asked if I wanted to start a band with him it was an obvious and immediate yes. It was soon apparent that saxophone was not the instrument that was needed for the music we were making so I switched to keyboards. Shortly thereafter we were joined by TJ Berry on guitar and vocals and we formed the band 94th Street. 94th Street was an amazing experience not only did I get to share the stage with two of best musicians I have played with; It was also some of the highest and lowest moments I would experiences as a musician. After all it was a band and being in a band is like family can't have the good without the bad. The musician I am today started to solidify in this band. Not only did I start playing keyboards but I also started singing and rapping. I realized that I not only wanted to perform but I wanted to "say" something. What I wanted to say, I wanted to be positive and hopefully give people something to think about.

This was when I met my wife; I am married and have two kids. I also use this band as a chance to raise awareness about autism. My son was diagnosed on the autistic spectrum, so in March of 2009 I started collecting donations at all my shows for Autism Speaks. I still played in bands but none of them really spoke to me the way 94th Street did. Until at the end of 2008 I decided to go "solo", and I formed the band I am in today, theZim & Arock. theZim & Arock is all my music and I use it as a platform to say what I want to say and present through music the messages I believe in. In theZim & Arock I play guitar, harmonica, sing and rap, I feel like I have found my musical home.

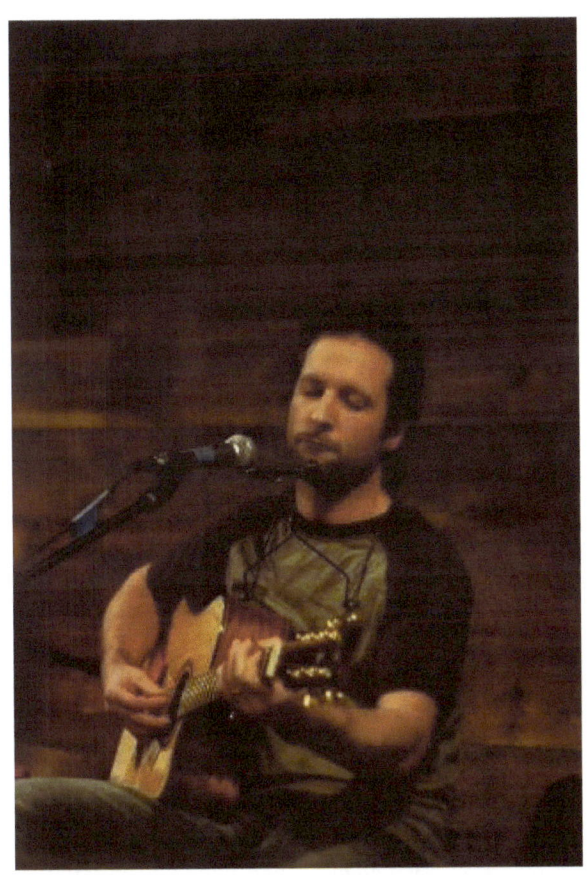

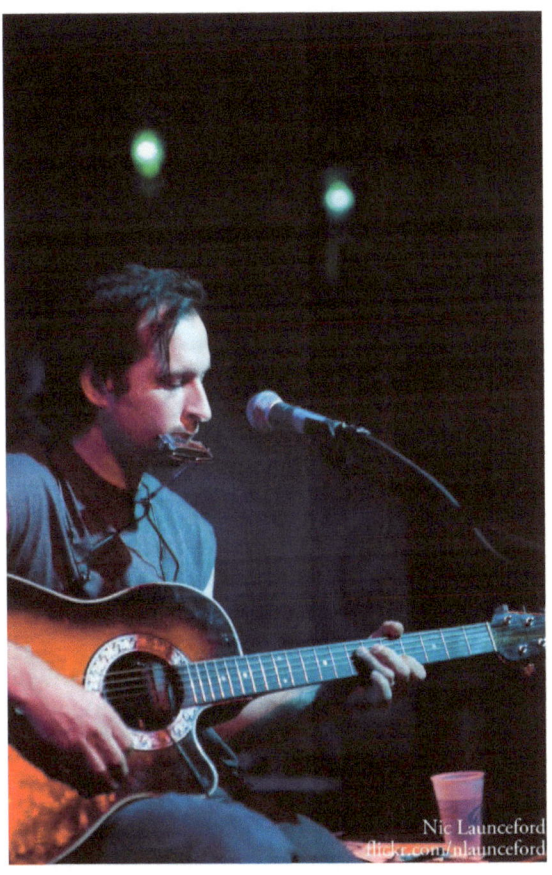

Nic Launceford
flickr.com/nlaunceford

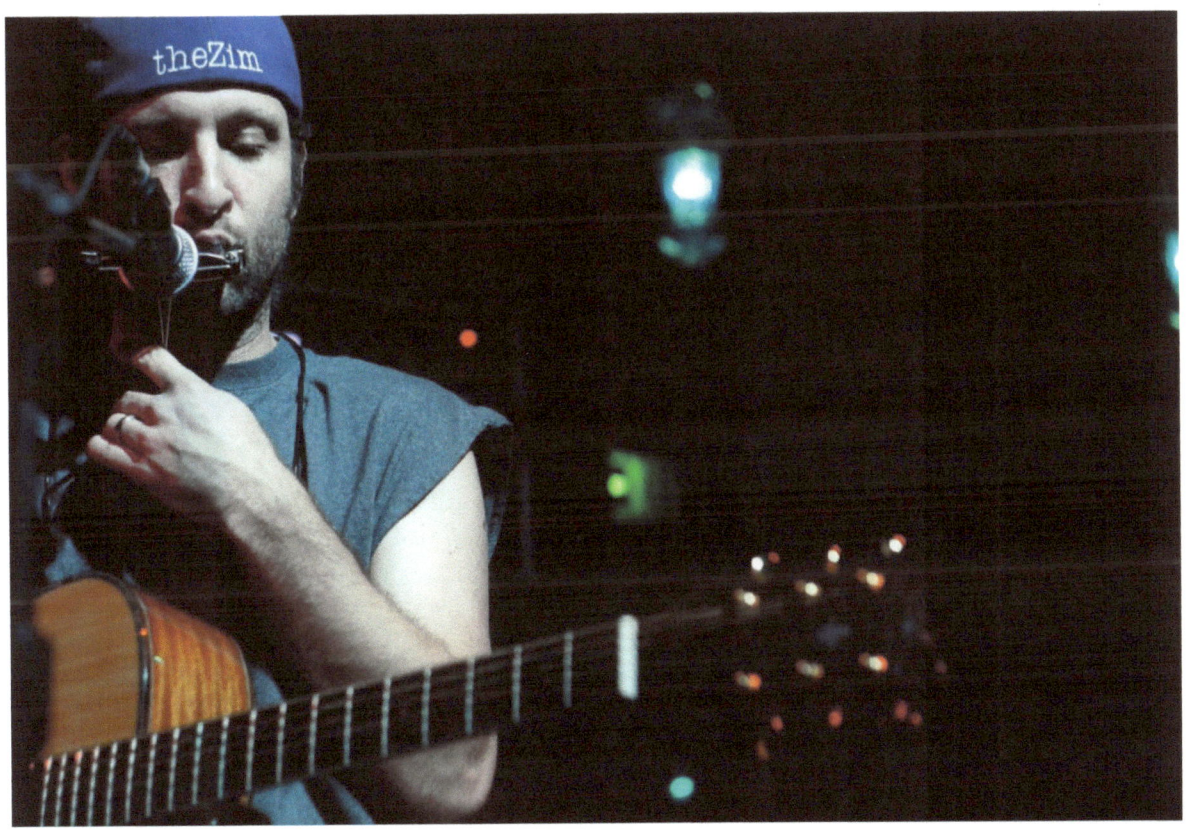

Alex Zimmerman

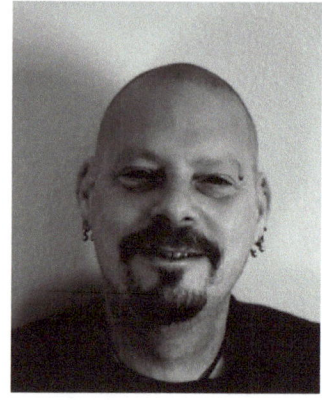

Bruce Webber

As a child I suffered to an extensive degree from ADHD. The only two things that could keep me in one spot for more than a few minutes were music and art. I spent hours at times looking through my mother's art books and would examine every detail. Another fascination was finding patterns in everyday things such as carpets, wood grain and sidewalk cracks.

My mother and Aunt both drew and painted. My father was a realist. He never cared for abstract art and told me that if I was going to draw to "draw something real." This affected my views on drawing and narrowed the way I looked at art.

Through school I became more interested in other art forms such as poetry, music and drama and all but gave up any visual form of creation. While busy with a lot of activities during this time I started to suffer from mild depression. I wanted to do something helpful. I entered nursing school after high school. I worked in a lot of high stress areas such as E.R. and cardiology.

While fulfilling in many ways there was very little if any room for creativity. This only served to exacerbate the depression further. Needing a diversion I bought a camera and later a scanner then discovering that the photos could be manipulated, everything lying around got scanned and combined with photos.

I began posting on Usenet groups and found that there were people that actually liked what I created. Submitting work to different art sites and occasionally being featured kept me motivated. I moved to Washington in January of 1999 planning to take a year off work to focus on art.. The beauty of this state inspired me to take up permanent residence. I greatly enjoyed the trees, mountains and being able to visit the ocean when opportunity presented.

I create for myself for the most part. I find it helps with working out stress. It's extremely cathartic and gives me a sense of calmness similar to meditation. I focused on trying to learn more about photo manipulation and the software that I used I enjoy all types of art and draw inspiration from the classics to the many artists who are present throughout the Internet community.

The best advice that I can offer to others is work hard, follow your vision regardless of what others think and keep an open mind. Don't be too critical of others, they're trying to achieve the same goals as everyone else.

Peace and love to all,

Bruce

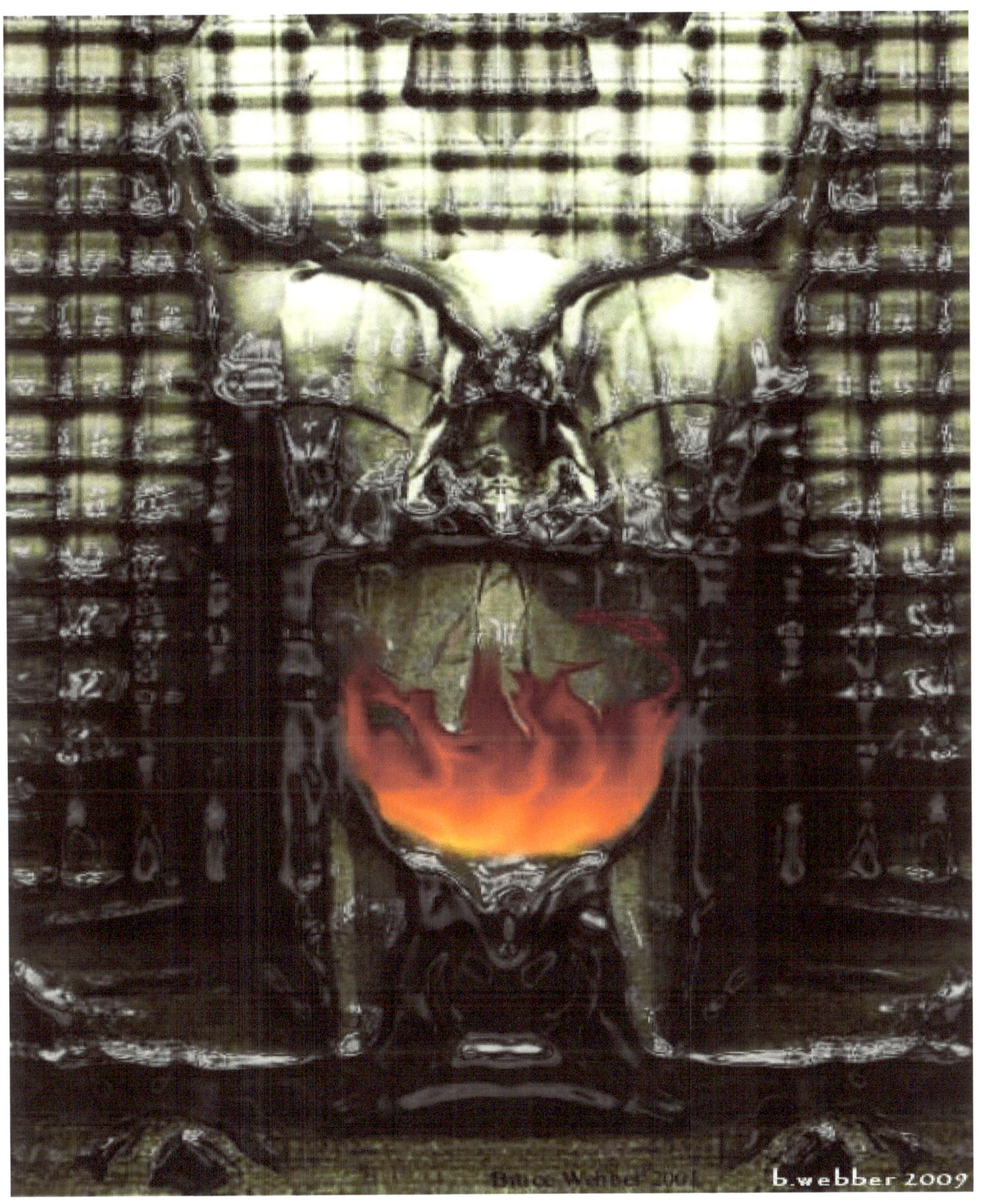

"Furnace" Bruce Webber

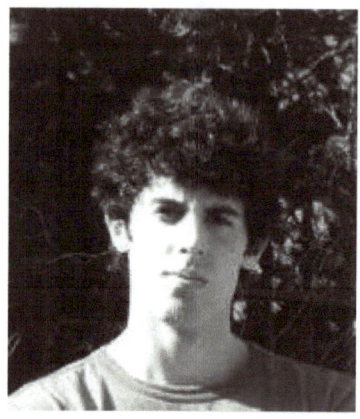

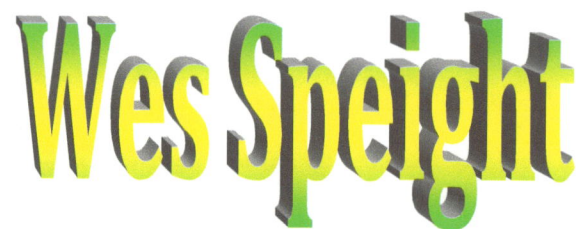

As early as I can remember from my childhood, I can still hear my Mother putting on the "Meet the Beatles" record on the turntable. Listening to that record had a huge impact on my life. I was born in and raised mainly in Tennessee, though my younger sister was born in Dallas Texas, where my family lived for a short time. I found music at an early age at my Grandparents house in Chattanooga TN, where they encouraged me to play piano. My parents bought me a drum kit when I was 15, and shortly after I picked up a guitar and started teaching myself.

I had always loved poetry and could fill up a notebook writing in no time. Playing guitar and piano expanded my poetry into songwriting and it quickly became an obsession and passion. I moved from Chattanooga to Nashville to get more involved in music in any way shape or form that I could. In college I studied audio engineering, and learned that while I did enjoy engineering, I was much more comfortable as a recording/performing musician. I began to play shows in Nashville and experimenting with sound and songwriting.

I found a producer/engineer named Jon Stinson who at the time, was working with some musician friends of mine. I contacted Stinson and asked him if he would be interested in producing/engineering some songs that I wanted to record. At the time, Stinson was busy with other projects, and about a year later we recorded the Please EP which was released through an independent media label founded by Jon Stinson called Radical Notion.

After continuing to promote the Please EP and play several shows in Nashville, I decided it was time to make a move. I booked a couple of shows in Seattle towards the end of 2008, to see what the Seattle scene was like and if I felt like Seattle could be the place to go. Upon playing the shows, the response I received was evident that I needed to get away from Nashville for a while and try a new surrounding and it has been a wonderfully life changing experience for me. I have thoroughly enjoyed my time thus far in Seattle, and the music scene here seems to be eclectic and inviting. After we recorded the Please EP and began promoting it, I was interested in radio play to reach a broader audience. We were successful in getting radio play in Nashville and Stinson and I did two live interviews on WRVU 91.1FM. I was the featured artist on lightning 100 100.1FM on two occasions which is a 50watt station. I only state the success we had with radio to explain that currently my goal is no longer to reach out to radio for airplay or really any kind of public media.

It's quite obvious that the music industry is changing everyday and there are almost endless ways to reach a broad audience via digital media independently. Today I can say that I am first interested in making music to make music, not to achieve mass media success or make millions of dollars, or even have the media tell you how to think or feel about my music.

Music is emotion open for interpretation. Making music today you have to be innovative, open, and radical if you want anything to happen. My advice to anyone and everyone who is making music is to do it because you are passionate about it. Do it because it makes you happy, or because it sparks emotion and makes you feel something in a way that you cannot duplicate. Don't be motivated by money or anything else. Money will come as long as you are persistent, passionate, and efficient with your time and creativity. Do whatever it takes to make music happen, tomorrow isn't promised so don't wait till the time is right, the best time is now.

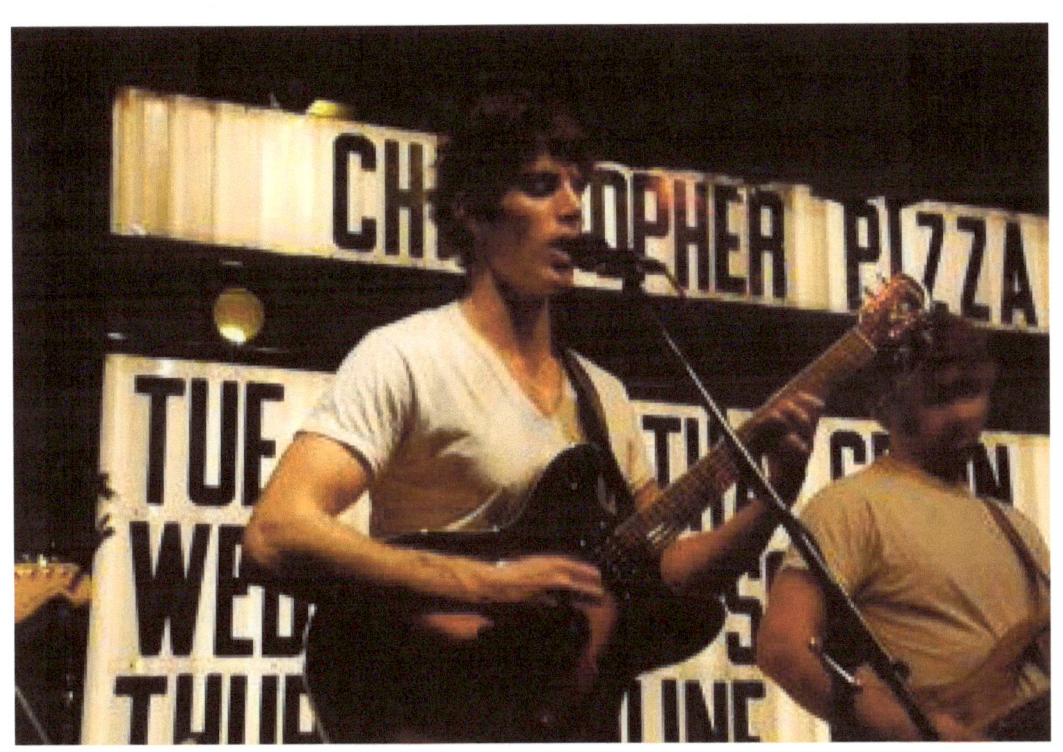

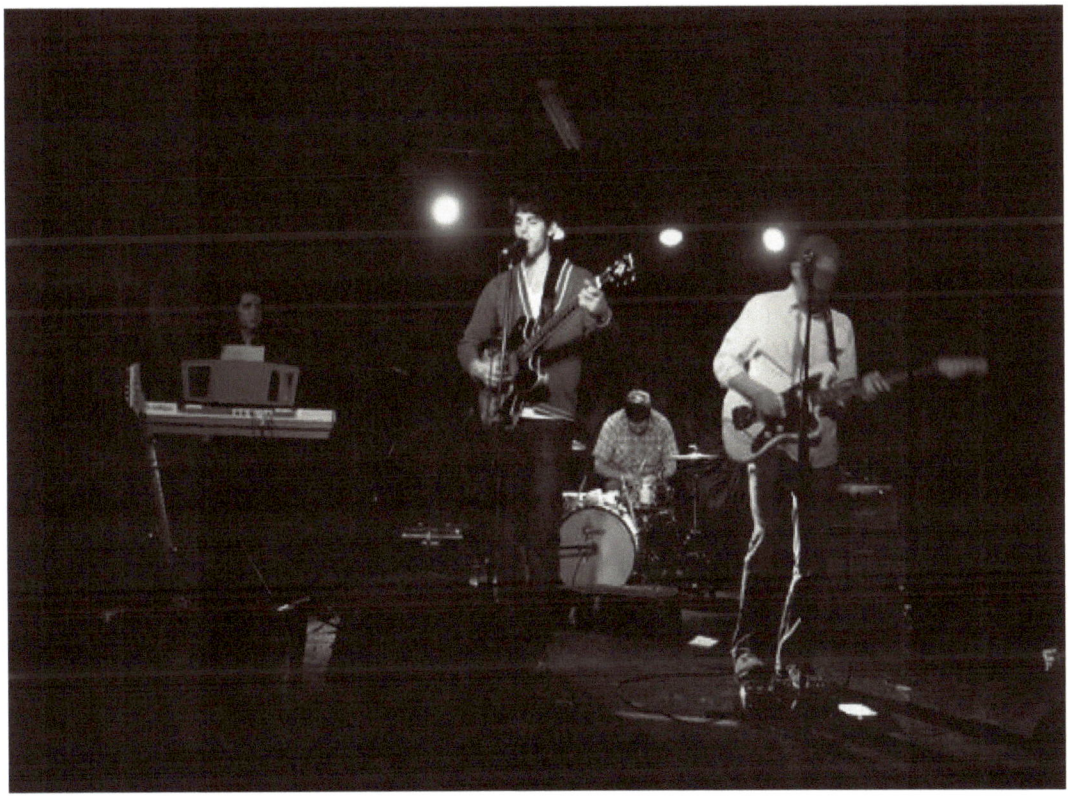

Wes Speight

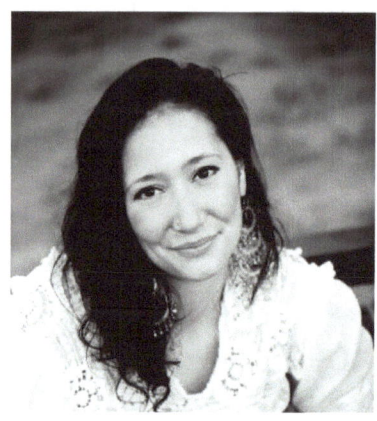

Jessica Bowler

Take advice from someone who failed art class. And truth be told the teacher can't be blamed for my inability to draw or show up to class on time. None of the less in high school my art teacher scoffed at my work. In collage I wish I could say I finally got the support I was looking for but I distinctly remember the comment, "you can paint but so what."

So what?

So all my life I shouldn't have been an artist or writer. I couldn't draw and my reading comprehension was very low. But Shakespeare said, "Necessity is the mother of invention." And necessity in this case was my insatiable desire to create- that is all I needed... that and the ability to play. The desire to create, and a spirit of playfulness, bridged the gap and allowed me to do what I wouldn't have otherwise because of how my brain was wired.

Playfulness is paramount... it allows me to let the subconscious go to free creativity and non-judgment, to open doors and make connections I didn't know were there.

Diane Ackerman noted in her book, "Deep Play" that in Anglo-Saxon, play was *plega* which meant singing dancing clapping, but also inferred something of a risk, chance, and to expose oneself to hazard. There was danger and peril in play as well.

In art there is always the danger of creating something "unworthy", of ruining your work or being criticized. But with great risk often comes great reward. So what? So there are always challenges and obstacles. Be thankful for being forced to look at the world and art differently. Don't focus on the negative voices around and the reasons why you "can't" simply work hard play hard and enjoy the beauty of what you have achieved. Because it is beautiful!

ABOUT THE ART: A medley of wax, tissue,

Decorative papers, photography, found objects and acrylic paint- my compulsion to create led me to adapt collage by making printed tissue transparent with wax, resulting in layer rich art. Because of the layers, my art is best viewed close and far, so subtle details can be noticed.

Art allows me delve into the terrains of the body, capturing dream landscapes of hair, neck, face and chest. I pin each image down like a bug in a collection box, or the curve of a road on a map; to be searched and recognized, and to lead, point by point to the possibility of a destination, of discovery. My art has the same grab-you-by-your-collar enthusiasm as my poetry, and the same expression of geography in a luminal space.

My art reflects this raw emotion and intense passion. Because my art has such a strong link with my emotions it often delves with my own personal/physical geography and history. It is this understanding of my compulsion that led me to pursue art to the fullest at Cornish College of the Arts, in Seattle, and Fairhaven Collage at Western Washington University in Bellingham where I graduated in 2007.

Currently I am creating art in a very small shack in my fiancés back yard. I have become inspired by found objects and rummaging through things found at abandoned houses. I have incorporated old ivory piano keys, recovered rotting picture frames, half destroyed guitars into my art and it has transformed the aesthetic of my work. I enjoy giving new life to discarded things, and the surprise objects that scavenging provides really pushes my work! I am pushing my art to be more narrative and poem like in its story telling- I've been using old family photos and adding magical real elements to give old stories new life and I'd like to continue to weave meaningful dreams and symbols in my work.

Giving art to those who can't afford it is a priority of mine as well. Art should be valued and accessible and I do my best to give back to my community by donating work. My goal is to live off of my art while maintaining the purity of creating art for art's sake. And if that doesn't happen I will settle for simply creating in the privacy of my very small shack at a feverish rate!

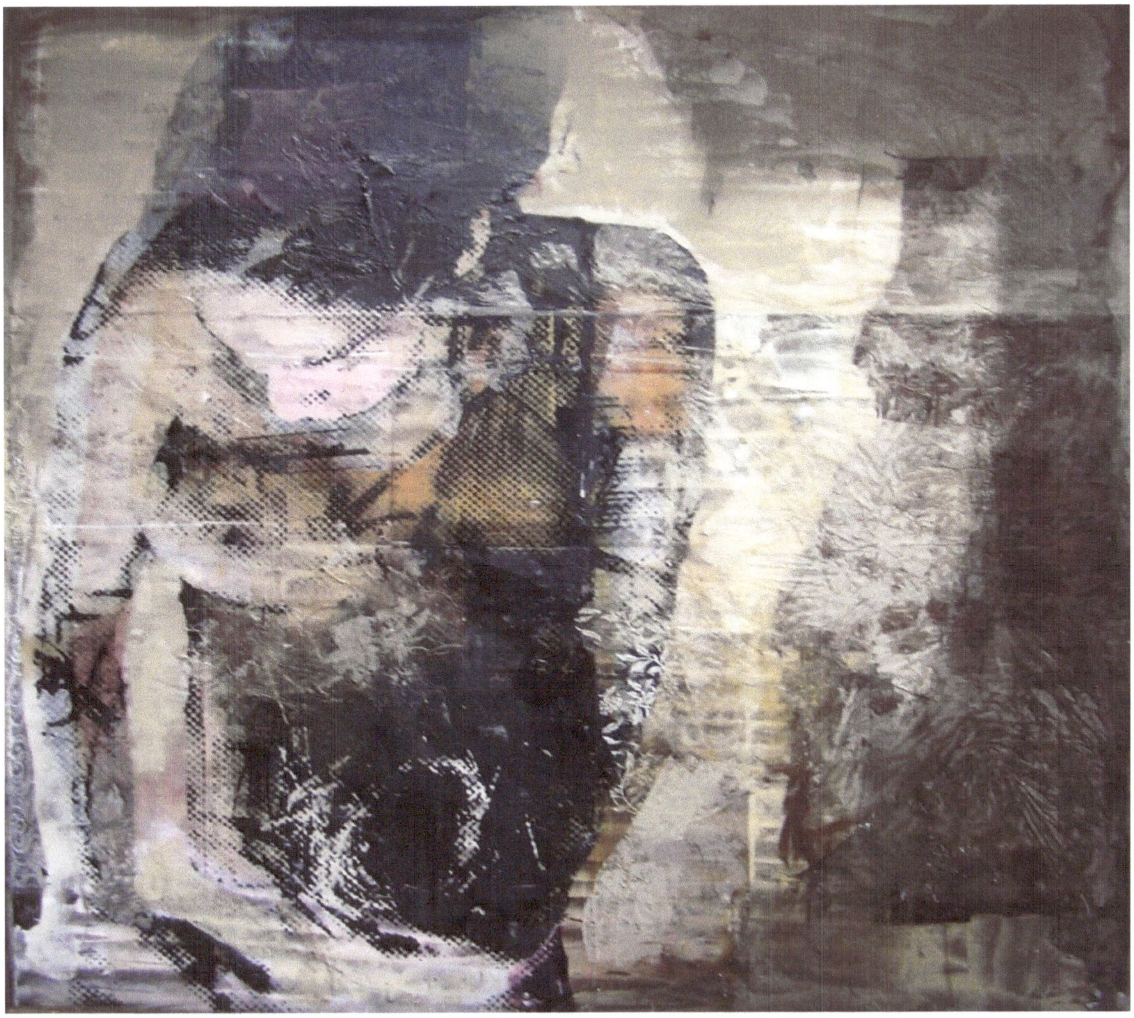

"You and Your Nest" Jessica Bowler, 2008 Mixed Media 32x44"

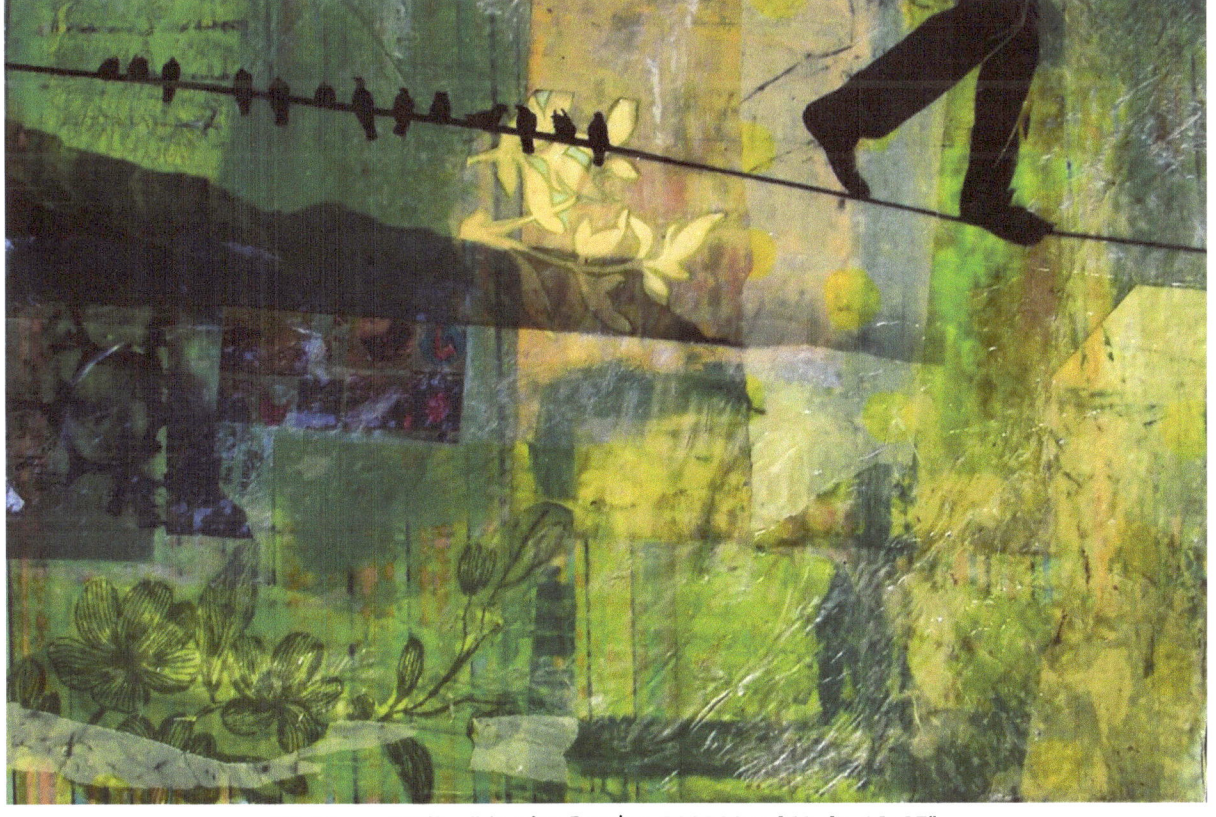

"Tightrope Walker" Jessica Bowler, 2008 Mixed Media 18x27"

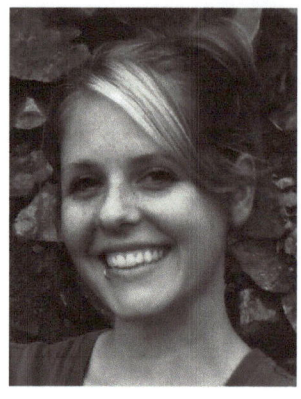

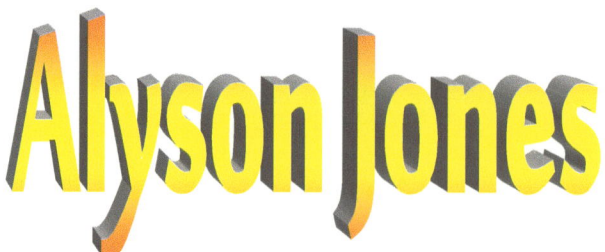

I am an artist because I have passions for creating and problem solving. From start to finish, each work is its own unique, visual puzzle! The artist must use their creative sense to bring innovation and individuality to their work. I find this process extremely rewarding; not everyone has the opportunity to create on a daily basis!

When I first began painting, the concept behind my work was: realistic and capturing. As an artist who mainly paints from photographs, I was determined to find photos that were both beautiful and inspiring. As a result, I began taking a variety of portrait and landscape commissions. It wasn't until these last few years that I decided to further develop my personal style and content. Currently, I am working on a surreal or dream-like series titled: "Phantasmagoria: Challenging the Real". I hope to bridge the gap between dream and reality by painting "realistic" fantastical scenes. I've learned to further explore content and composition so viewers can lose themselves within each piece.

In my opinion, mood and emotion are extremely important for successful artwork. Never have I begun a painting before visualizing the viewer's reaction to the finished piece. Will they view the work and pass on by? Or will they stand and admire, exploring the meaning and story beyond the canvas? Movement, gaze, color, texture, or position; when properly illustrated, these (and many other) visual elements evoke both mood and emotion. As an artist, I feel that it is my duty to enable this visual response.

Sometimes an idea for a composition will come at the most random of times. It is important, therefore, that I carry with me a small notepad or journal. I also find it useful to always carry a camera. A camping trip, a conversation, or perhaps, even a walk can inspire an element for an upcoming painting; it's important to allow your mind to work at will. Once I have these notes or photographs, I begin the brainstorm process. Sometimes this involves a drawing pad, while other times this involves manipulating photos on my computer. All of my most recent paintings in the Phantasmagoria series have begun from a photo composited image. An image, therefore, that has been spliced together from a variety of other images or drawn elements. These photo-composites allow me to work out the piece completely before even touching the canvas. Perhaps it's my design background, but I feel the computer offers me brainstorm capabilities that no pen and paper can do.

The role of the artist is to generate creative stimuli. Anything that inspires, arouses, or simulates; it is the artist's duty to find a unique and innovative means of communication. No matter the medium, the artist must establish a connection to the viewer. They are the igniter and producer of creativity. In Washington, as in all other locations, artists enable viewers a recess from reality. Artwork desires in the big city of New York, for example, differ from those existing in the smaller town of Leavenworth, WA. It is the artist's duty to recognize these desires and to bring a individually, unique flare to that environment.

I would love to show all over the U.S. and in Europe. I hope to gain exposure over the next few years and further develop the uniqueness of my artwork. It would be wonderful someday to own a gallery and teach painting and drawing lessons. I also am hoping to publish another art-related book sometime in the next few years.

Art is a creative means for expression. I am a lover of fantasy and a nightly dreamer! Reveries can become reality! I am fascinated by the process of creation and by the ability to inspire and excite the viewer. Producing art quells my analytical and problem-solving desires; it allows me to visually express my fantastical obsession! I can be goofy, weird, or nostalgic, and then put it all down on canvas. Above all, it makes me feel important, successful, and happy!

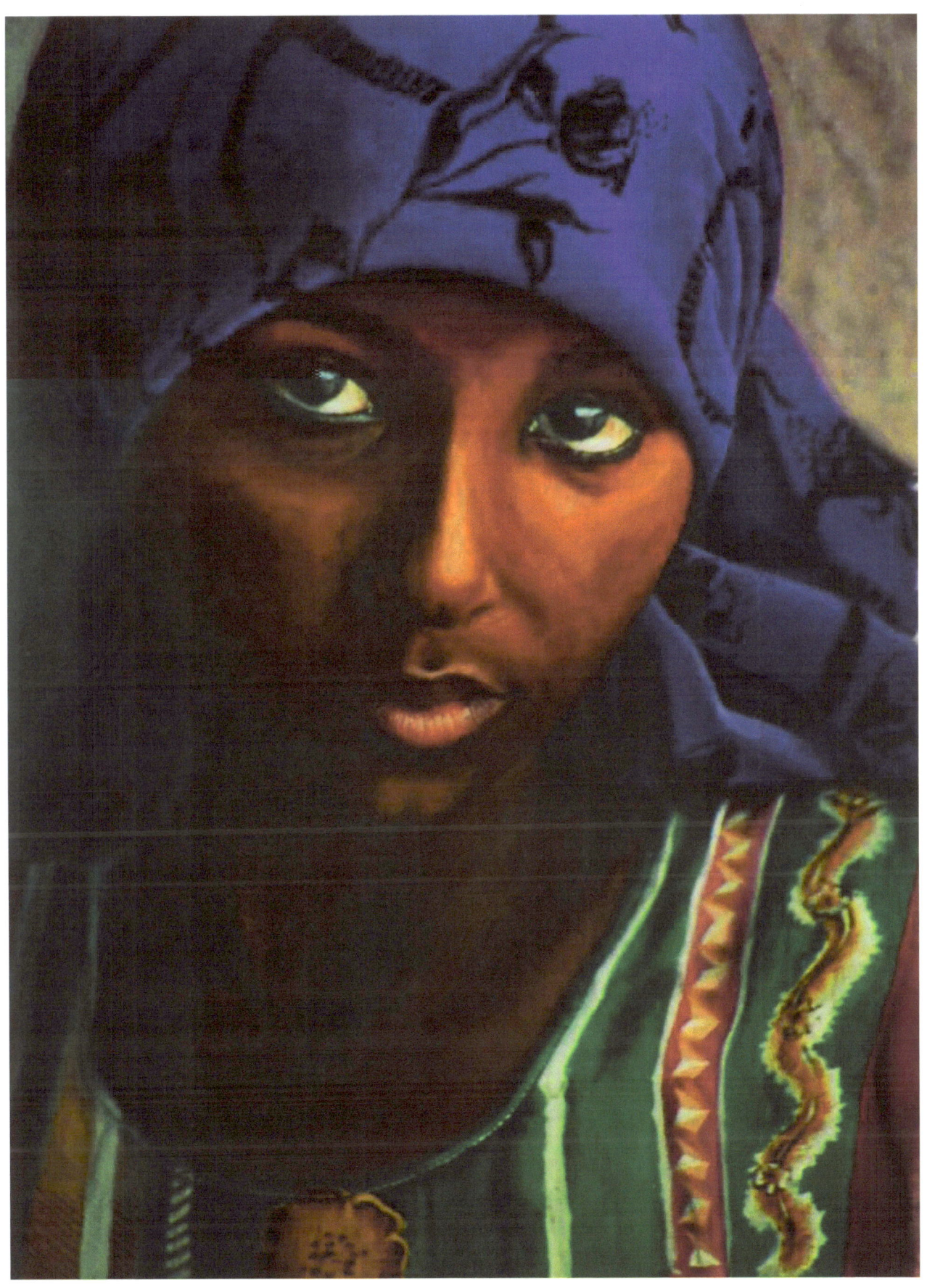

"Woman of Sanaa" Alyson Jones, Acrylic on Canvas, 2001

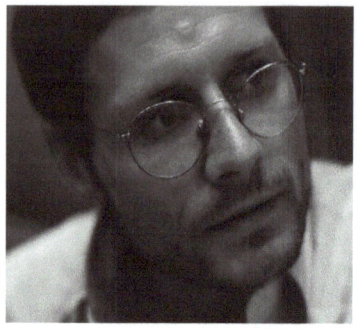

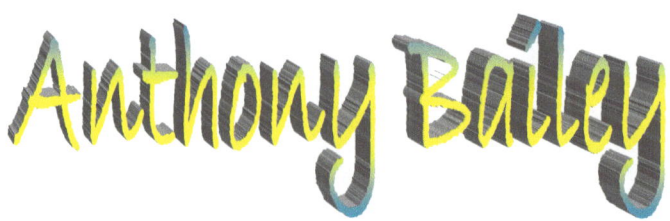

I've heard that when a family member dies on your birthday you inherit their knowledge.
My Grandma, who insisted on being called Nana Jackie, was self-taught in homeopathy, energy theories and pendulum polarity. She died on March 24, 1998, my seventeenth birthday.

Years later, I began to understand what she knew in unexplainable fashion. It was like sleeping with a book under the pillow and the next morning acing a test. The knowing without studying felt the most powerful. Her notes and journals fell into my hands and I dove further into the rare art of pendulum polarity. Learning of the energy humans possess and harness fascinated me and with it a gift to blend new and old thinking.

I learned to use the exercises of natural healing and incorporated it into how I make art. My newly opened chakras and meridians allowed me to put away anger and resentment, focusing on the happiness that the process of art created within. The flow, or lack thereof, of energy corresponded to my artistic thoughts and productivity. Healing myself with natural ways put my mind and body into a constant trance like state, where I meditated on all things.

Subsequently, I began to break down my art like a pitcher would break down his delivery, specifically in music. I went through a two year period where I would rarely write a song to completion. I never settled on a specific; chorus or verse of words, melodies or music. I continued to play live but would improve my way through sets. My concerts began to take on a performance art vibe, where the audience would be confused when the songs stopped or began. I did not mean to be rude in that manner, I felt separated from the audience but in a comforting way.

Making live music has been my most passionate of art forms in 2009. I did not record very much of my work, but not for lack of want. I am incredibly lacking in resources compared to most musicians I know. Though, every show I played I went with tape recorders and video cameras. Sometimes getting so involved in the performance I would forget to press record or I experienced technical difficulties. The tapes I do have I value very much, one for the history they contain and as a reference for future learning.
I am interested in art that is emotionally expressive. I want to be able to read the artists' thoughts, future and past by viewing or listening to their work. Nor do I believe that art needs an audience to become alive and real, an audience other than oneself. It is art before the pen strikes the page, the moment the electricity fires inside.

The advice I get from most people is to pick one thing and stick with it, make it your specialty. That is what I struggle with most. I am torn which direction to go sometimes. Devote myself to helping other people through natural healing or sharing my art with them? Each one needing more pure energy and devotion to find it's absolute potential. I do not want to be a musician or artist on the side, I want to expand from the center.

I work with music, photography, video, journalism, painting, drawing, performance and poetry.
My art is based on free flowing thoughts, the collected subconscious and a search for the fourth dimension. The subconscious could be what some people refer to as karma. Whereas the fourth dimension is that place we cannot see but exists everywhere, the active present energy.

I go through multiple processes when creating art. I constantly pose enquiry into the art phenomenon, I want to play with it. Being described as one that 'believes in uninhibited thoughts and the ridiculous', self-doubt is a mindset I rarely suffer from. I have complete confidence in my abilities. I urge everyone to combine their own excellence in standards and letting what happens flow. I'm reminded of the title from Anna Hoovers' first art show, 'What comes naturally.'

I view recognizable similarities in my art as signs of staleness, a fear of growth. To counter this, I review my art in all stages and will work on a drawing, against my nature, for several years. Though, the quick shutter of a lens apparatus is less forgiving. When I begin to recognize patterns in my art. I ask, have I become stale? Or is it the strength of the subconscious' story asking to be told?

Break every stereotype you've ever heard about an artist. Live like you'd imagine a poet would three thousand years ago, pondering the way dust floats through the sky. Wallow in the days when the redwoods were at their peak and the nights when the moon told stories, share yourself through art.

I believe in the Hunter S. Thompson shibboleth; 'Art as Life'.

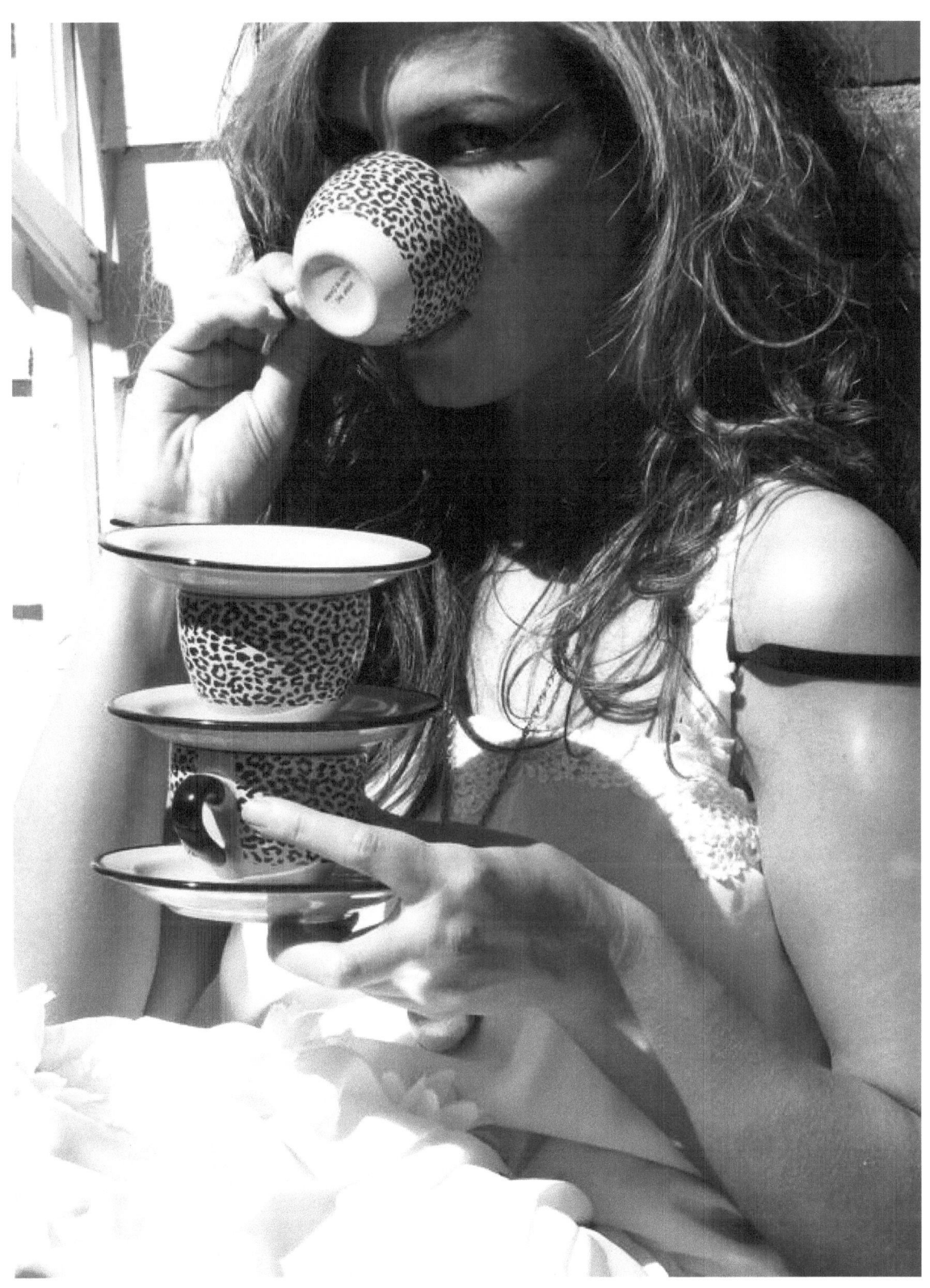

"Cup of Tea" Anthony Bailey, Digital Photograph, 2008

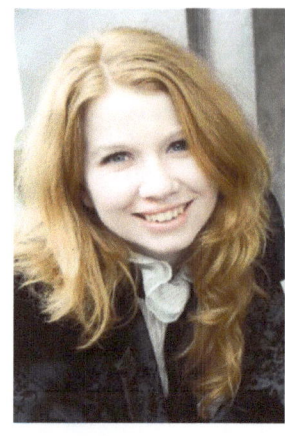

Sarah Harris

Taking ownership of being an artist has been the hardest struggle of my career. I viewed the title as a box that didn't fit right. It wasn't until a friend in college pointed out that being an artist was not exclusive to other things and that it is being many things. All ideas stem from creativity and the artist helps inspire the movement and growth of creativity. Creativity is the breath in life of which we live.

After graduating with an art degree, I started out as an archaeological illustrator. It was one of the most thrilling and rewarding jobs I have yet to experience. However, it is also a nomadic lifestyle and decided after a couple years it wasn't what I wanted in the long run if I was to have a relationship, etc. I came to a crossroads shortly after, and a friend asked me, "What can't you live without?...then check off the list."

Making clothes and drawing were the top two on my list. It was then that I realized my passion for fashion, drawing, and all the elements behind the process of designing a garment. I walk into a fabric store and feel as you can imagine Audrey Hepburn's character at Tiffany's in "Breakfast At Tiffany's". I started out making bridal wear for friends and eventually evolved into producing my own line: more day-to-night dresses and special occasion.

Once I decided to become a fashion designer, the hardest struggle in the field is not having a degree. My mother had taught me to sew at a young age which I followed with self teaching, but no matter how impressive my portfolio was - I could not get hired without a degree in the field. That's what inspired me to start my own company with lots of books to rely on.

Over the years, I have learned copious amounts about the business of fashion. But, at the end of the day, my evolution as a designer is an exploration much in the manner of an artist. I explore different materials, techniques, and create garments which I believe to credit beauty, inspire, create a mood, and are personal to the woman wearing them. I think as an artist, this approach transforms a garment from a fashion item to something personal and therefore, more enjoyable to wear.

When photographing my garments, I enjoy presenting them in a story and environment that is seemingly unlike the garment as a standalone piece. I try to walk the line between creating a wearable garment and presenting it with an artful explanation or storyline. I draw inspiration from Cindy Sherman in this way.

Being a fashion designer in Seattle is a challenge; however, rewarding just the same. The largest obvious challenge is the perception that functional clothing cannot equal beautiful clothing. However, the fashion community here is dedicated to keeping good fashion local. Many support local independent designers and aren't compelled to wear big name designers. This allows smaller designers like me to distribute to boutiques who fully support local talent. That is inspiring and shows a lot of promise for the designer community here.

Above all that I've learned is – create, create, create, and then create some more. The people I've known to succeed are not necessary the most talented, but the ones who are diligent at challenging themselves and working at it every day.

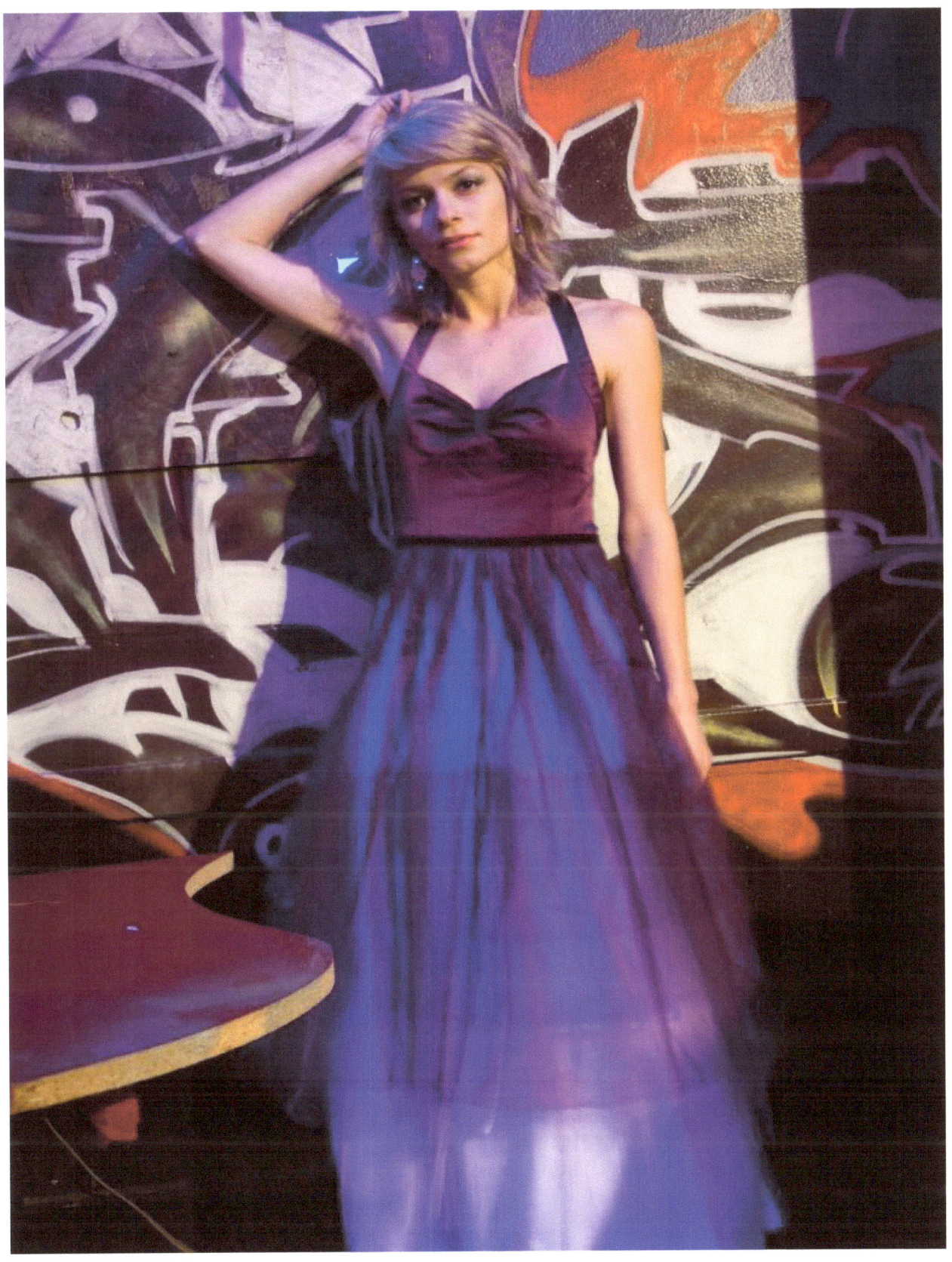

"Purple Duchess" Sara Harris, Silk 2009

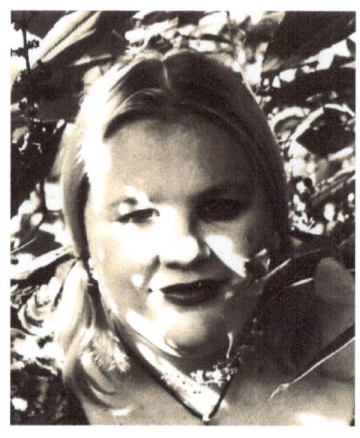

Molly Brewer

I've always been inspired by Art in all its forms. It started when I was a young child with a deep connection to music, books, movies and other visual arts. These opened up worlds to me of infinite possibilities and a means of momentarily leaving what seemed to be, at times, a painful and accusing world. They also conjured feelings from within that were both exciting and somehow safe for me. I began writing and drawing in my early teens and into my young adulthood, but was always too self-critical and self-protective to share my creations with others.

Everything changed in 2000 when I saw an image in my mind's eye that couldn't be drawn. I knew it must be painted, and even though it was a path I'd never walked before, I had to get this image on canvas. I gathered a little knowledge about acrylic painting and decided the best route to take was to just "jump in with both feet." As I became more experienced with the medium, my confidence grew. I did my first public showing in the autumn of 2001 and was astounded and filled with joy at the positive responses I received from the people viewing my Art. This gave me the needed push to explore the next level of my Artistic path, even before I could comprehend what it was or where it would lead.

Along with my interest in Art, I had a deep love and fascination with all things of a Metaphysical and Esoteric nature, anything that related to the growth of my Soul. In 2003 I decided to merge these two loves and create a Tarot deck. At the time I was being heavily inspired by a Canadian rock group called The Tea Party. Their music was a heady mix of other-worldly sounds and lyrical, esoteric ideas which I knew would lend the perfect foundation on which to build my Tarot images. The process was – see which song I was drawn to most at that moment, listen to the song over and over and paint what came to me. As I started the first painting (a song called "Emerald") I began to feel a new element to the song that had never entered my awareness. I found the painting I was creating was emerging as a reflection of a part of myself that thus far in my life had never had a voice. Emotions surfaced that had long been buried and I knew this was going to be more than a Tarot deck; this was going to be a processional catalyst for self-transformation and healing. This series of paintings continued to include 17 works, created from 2003 to 2005. Through the tears, the anger, the love and the growth generated by the process, I came out on the other side the closest to my true self I had ever been. I also emerged with the knowledge that experiencing and creating Art was a path to my growth and understanding of myself and my place in the world.

To this day, my Art continues to be a mirror to myself and my life, as well as a means of healing. I hope it is a catalyst for the same in others, much like the songs of The Tea Party and the other Art I've loved have been guides on the road of transformation for me. It is true, Art inspires Art inspires Art.

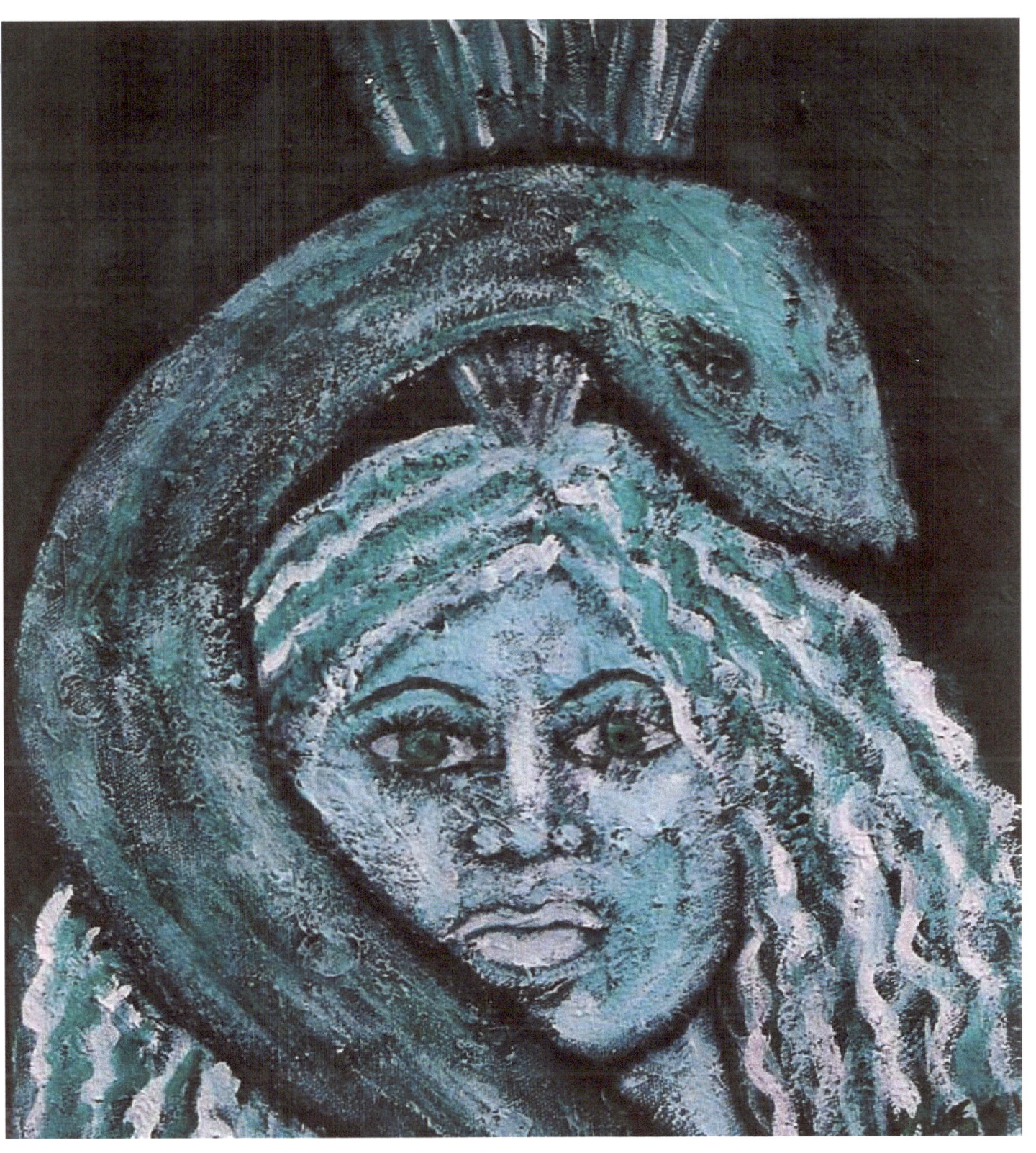

"Emerald" – Molly Brewer, Acrylics on 11x14 canvas. Date of creation - 2003

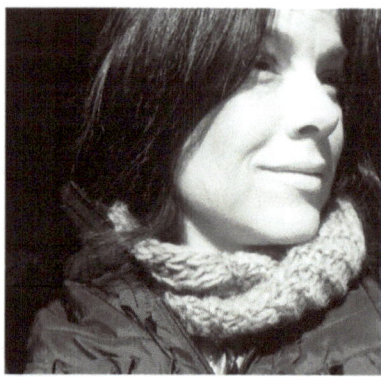

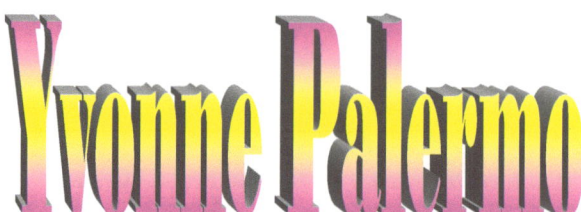

Ever since I was young my eyes always were drawn to the art world and the idea that what is in your mind can be translated through different art processes. I have since then, emerged myself in every aspect of learning the many different ways to create. Fiber arts, Printmaking, Sculpting, Foam sculpting, Jewelry, Scribbling, life drawing, glass fusing / sculpting, and painting are just some of the many techniques I treasure.

During one of my jobs as a foam sculptor I got the opportunity to create a massive sculpture for the Phoenix Zoo which led to creating many sculptures for some popular movie's and in turn found myself at one of my calmest moments in front of the camera booms being filmed for different shows on HGTV and DIY network television. I broke my neck and lower back in 1998, endured 30 surgeries, and through the chaotic process of being a patient with chronic pain, in the last eleven years, I have turned my scribbling into a feast of nude figure drawings.

The process of drawing in or out of the hospital was definitely my saving grace. Through the experience of being a patient I saw and learned more about my body and what lies under skin is so important to know for translating nude figures. I now am taking the imagery from my pain to canvas.

The body of work tells a deep story and I feel that it is imperative for art to have historical meaning behind every piece. I live art, I am art, I create art. Without having had walked through the threshold of pain and experiences of facing death, I would not have been able to find my unique trademark style which is critical to be an artist that captivates. I feel art should be something that grabs your soul that throws you into serenity, chaos, and pure emotional mayhem. To me that is what art does to a person when the art is pure.

Why I became an artist, truly to answer that, it is because I was born one. Everything inspires me, my pain, my courage, my fight to live, my will to create, and of course nature along with the human body is in itself art. I have had several struggles along with several accomplishments. They all serve a purpose, without them I would not be able to create what you see, feel, and contemplate upon.

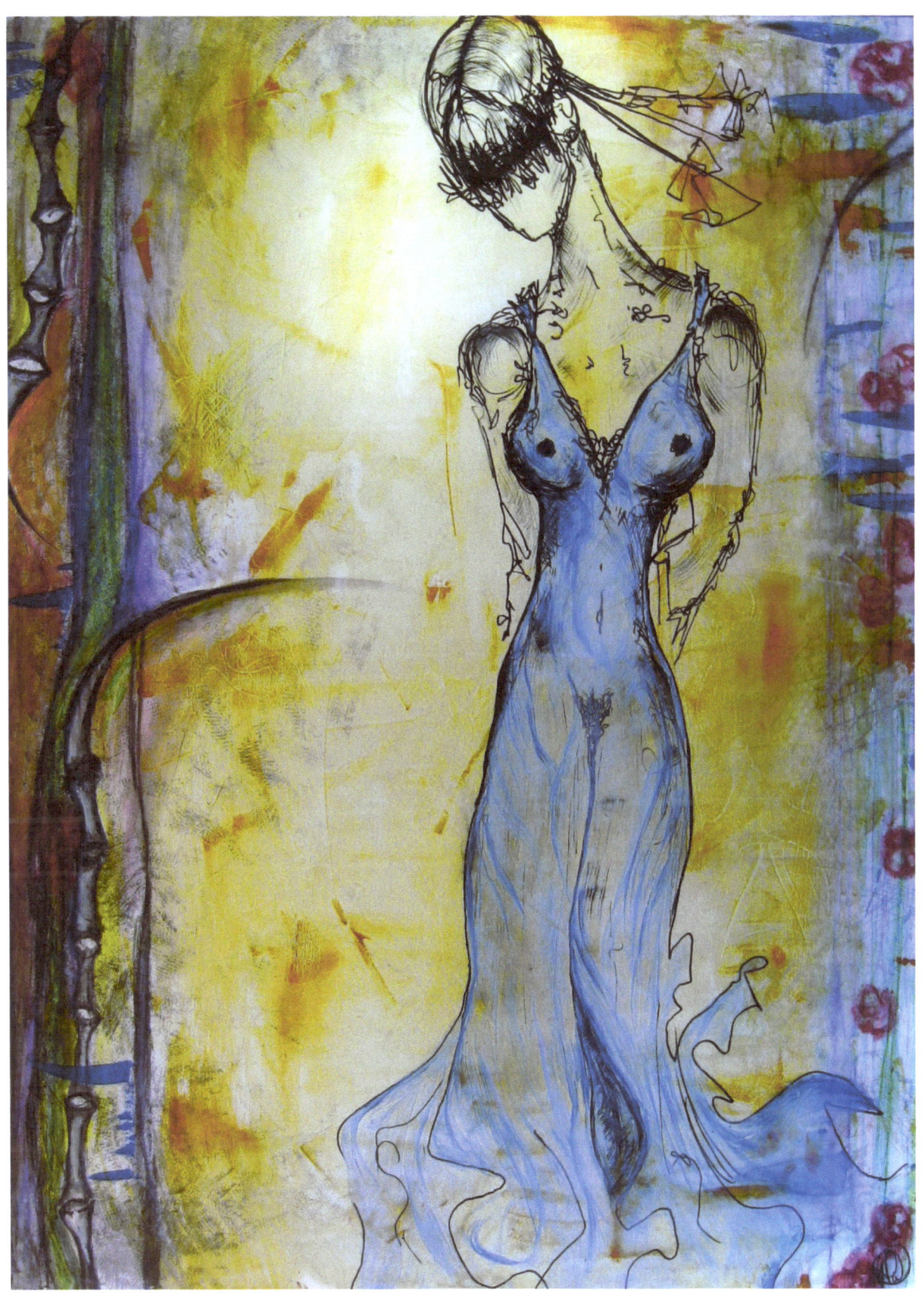

"Contemplation for growth" Yvonne Palermo   36X48, acrylic, 2008

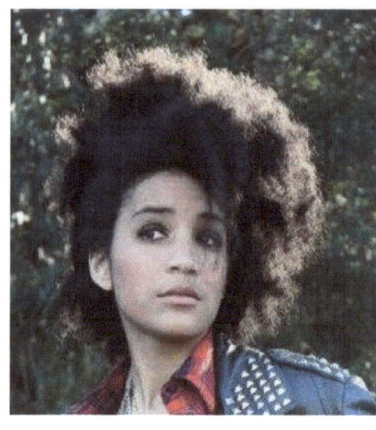

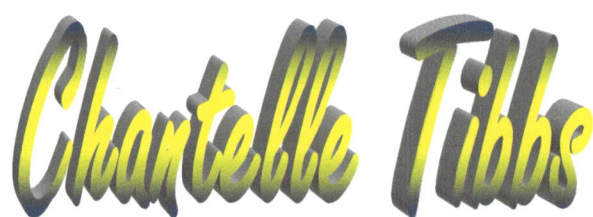

My father is a beautiful man. I don't say this as a disclaimer. He is the reason why I'm an artist. When I was a young girl I wanted so badly to be a ballerina. We were lower middleclass, the lottery winners of the classes. We were too rich for government assistance, and too poor to live. My mother offered time, and did office favors for the ballet companies I danced for in exchange for my dance lessons. In the middle of my ballet recitals my father would stand and scream "Go Chantelle!" as loud as he could.

Yeah, my dad was beautiful and loud. Unfortunately for my brother and I, my father was very unpredictable. We got yelled at a lot. I think writing music was a way to make the inside of my head quiet. When I focused on melodies and lyrics, I couldn't hear the slightly sharper and painful lyrics coming from my dad. I think it's why I write mostly quiet music too.

Joan Baez, and Sarah Mc Lachlan were two of my biggest inspirations growing up. I remember my first CD was a CD of Joan Baez's Greatest Hits. "Diamonds And Rust" was the first song I just couldn't stop listening to over and over and over again. I just got so wrapped up in the story and how the music was like an envelope for this moment Joan Baez lived through. I fell in love.

I think my biggest struggle was feeling like the music my heart wanted to play wasn't "black enough." R & B and Soul are some fabulous genres. But they aren't my genre. I joined an R& B group at 14. It didn't work out. I mean it took me forever to just let the whole racial image thing go. But at 20 years old I picked up a guitar and there was just no lying to myself anymore.

Another struggle was money. I had bad feelings about making it, selling myself and marketing altogether. I think it's sad that artistic people are pretty much encouraged to NOT make money. But that's not a way to live. I mean, literally. I always thought I was bad with numbers and businessy kind of stuff. Turns out I was wrong. Right alongside my musical accomplishments sits my music business successes. I absolutely enjoy accounting, and working through marketing strategies. I really just see it as a way to communicate to my audience. I enjoy finding new ways to surprise and spoil the people who listen to me. I have fun with it.

My goal is to be on the level of Mandy Moore. I'm also an actress and I appreciate how she balances both and picks good projects. So I'm aiming for her status, only Puerto-Rican, African American and Ambient/Indie/Folk. Tee hee.

I also started something called Money Be Green, where I give $50 to other artists for supplies and cost of living. I take 5% of my profits in music/acting and put it towards Money Be Green. My goal with Money Be Green is to be giving away $300k a year. That would help out 6,000 artists annually.

I think in order to be in a place to give advice I have to be fair and tell you where I'm at. If you want to be where I'm at then listen to me. If not, then I wouldn't. Lol. Advice is a tricky thing. So many people throw it out there, but if you don't want to wind up like the person giving it, then you should probably seek counsel elsewhere. So here it goes...

I haven't had a day job in over 2 years. Music and film/TV acting are what I do for a living. I cut down on expenses crazy style, so I could not be tied down in anyway, and get up and go whenever I need to. And all the money I do make 50% goes right back into my music business for tour and other expenses.

Advice...Get to marketing. But always, always make sure it's balanced with rehearsal and writing new material. Never think of this as a dream, MAKE it real. We get to shape our lives. Not everyone on this planet can say that. So just make it happen. Music is powerful. I feel like it's my job to get people out of their heads for even just a second. I take my job seriously. I think it's impossible to hit goals you don't see.

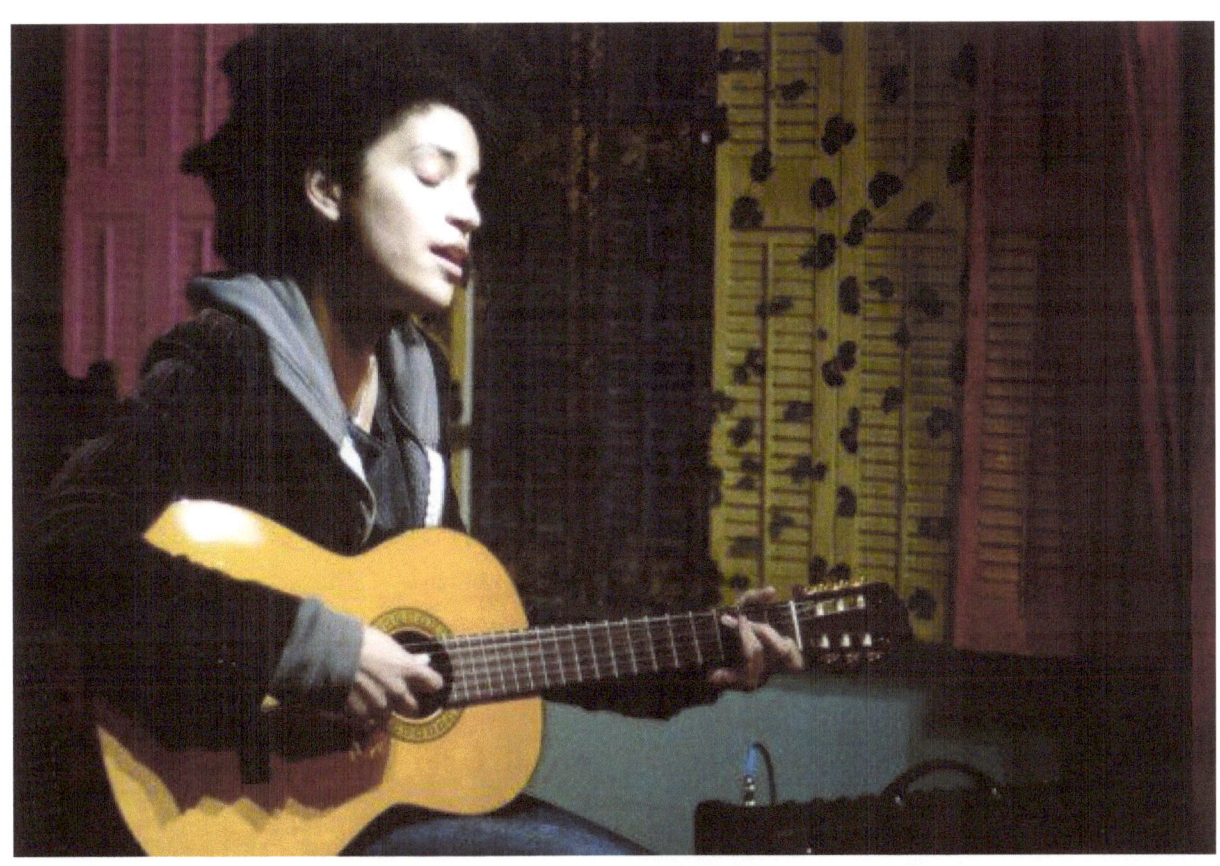

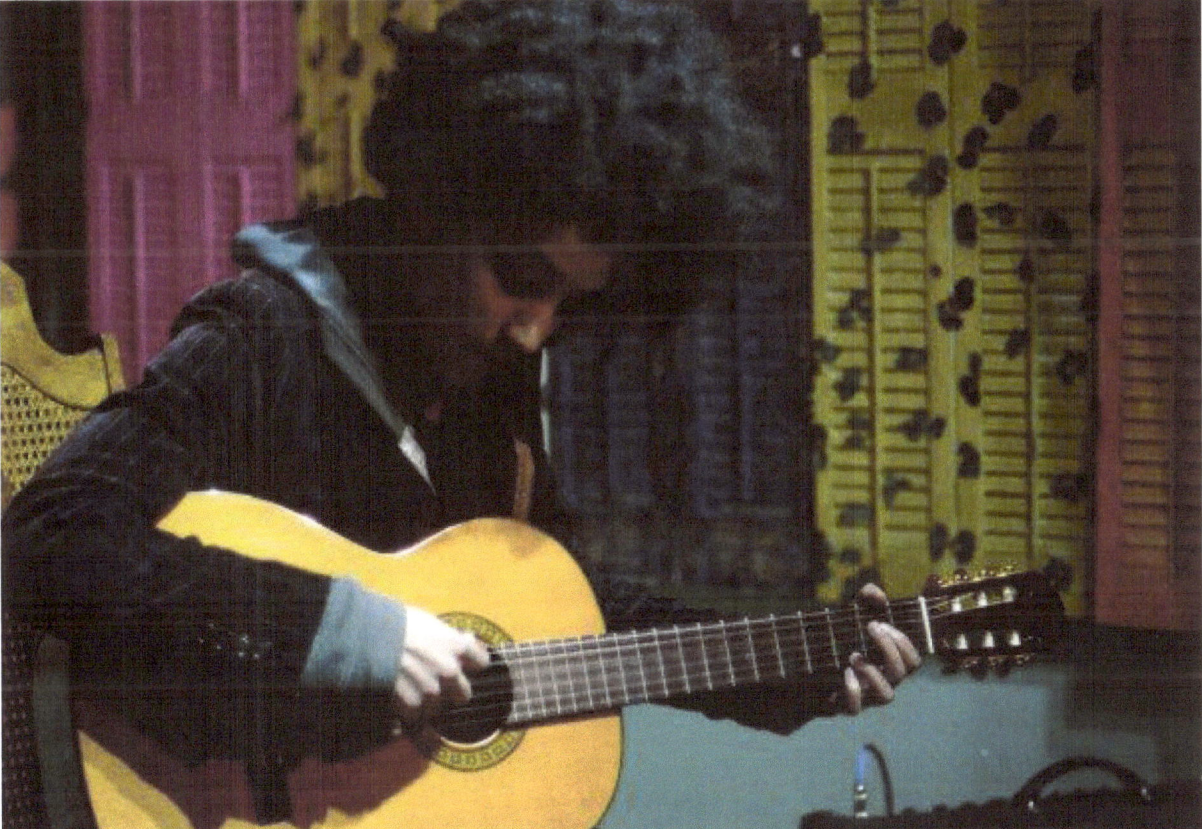

Chantelle Tibbs (Photography by Scott Finsthwait)

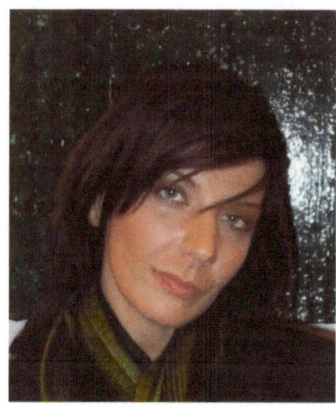
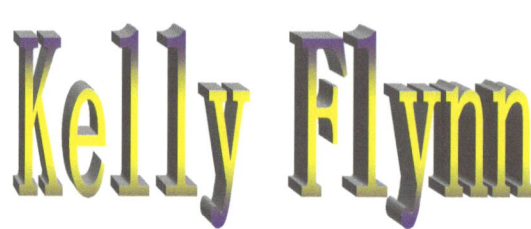

My name is Kelly Flynn. I was born on April 12, 1978 into the wild and desolate frontier of Montana and raised by working-class Irish hippies. My mother and father are full of character and love.

Using clothing as a means of expression became important to me at a very early age; my printed dog swimsuit took the place of a comfort blanket or teddy bear. I loved to model my different super-hero under-rue sets on my hot wheel and never wanted to leave the house without my star-shaped Bootsie Collins sunglasses. Fashion was a fun way to celebrate expression and individuality!

High school was as painful as a bad episode of *Flavor of Love*. Deprecating comments from one classmate to another were common practice and created self-esteem issues all around. I longed for a world where people could fall in love with themselves and their distinctive qualities through the exploration of style. There was something missing when I tried fit into a clique or conform to the norm. I used creativity to fulfill a void left by loneliness. I became inspired to sew, put together different looks, and paint on my porch underneath the vast, starry Montana sky. Watercolor fueled my appreciation for color and unique textures.

Hungry for change and the need to define myself, I set out to design and create clothing that exudes confidence, creativity, and innovation. I received a degree at the Art Institute of Seattle and have been passionate about style and design ever since.

My trademark style combines tailoring and handcrafted elements infused with an adventurous edge and modern fabrications. One of my goals is to create clothing unique enough to be worn through the seasons. I also love to bring together traditionalism and modernism.

I have persevered through the challenges presented by my professional path (tough in the best of times, potentially crushing during the current economic downturn), making personal sacrifices and putting in countless hours to perfect technique and advance a powerful creative vision.

Although I have received notice for my work, the greatest reward has been durable self-confidence and patience, and the ability to learn more every day. Design has blessed me with the ability to seek creativity in everything that I do. My dream remains to promote self expression, acceptance, and to captivate the spirit of my fashion clients.

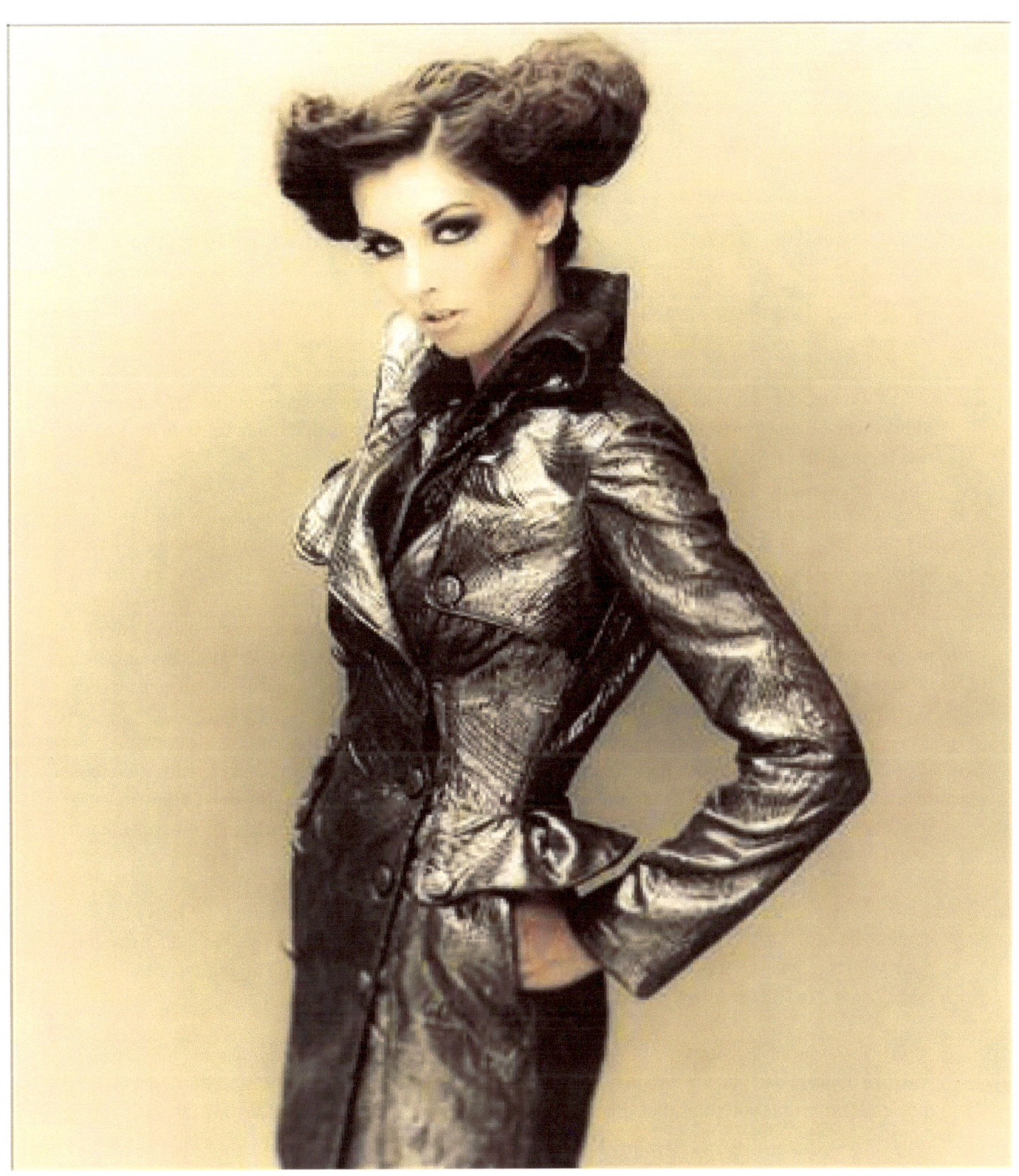

"Eleven-Eleven"   Kelly Flynn

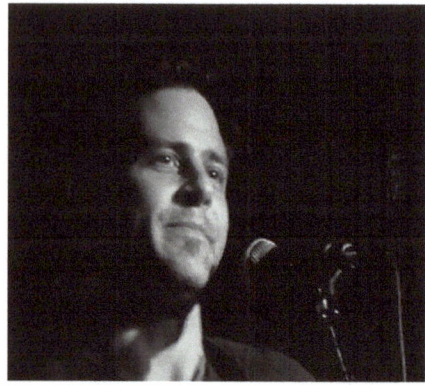

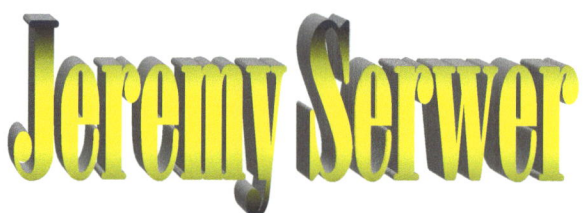

I realized music was my passion when singing into the stereo speakers at age 7 in Chicago Illinois. Then being impatient with lessons and wanting to write songs that made sense to me not what was theoretical.

My music keeps evolving and is highly influenced by the vibe of the Northwest. Rain and darkness play a large part of creative process and living in the desert proved to me how crucial it was in quality and productivity.

The music I create is eclectic; I have a hard time sticking to specific genres and am a fan of many styles. I would say I fit into the singer songwriter niche but with a few added twists and wanting bend genres. Some of my biggest musical influences are Elliott Smith, Jazz music, Nick Drake, Archer Prewitt, Air, King Crimson, Love, Calexico, Mike Patton, Richard Buckner

What makes my music unique is not having much of a theory or formal music education lends to taking chances with chord progressions. I'm out of the box but without trying to be. Many musicians with solid training are interested in the songs because of my unorthodox approach. However I'm not so out of the box that people don't get it.

Today, I quit a band that had a promising career and decided that I would from now on use my name to be heard. What's next for me is a new record with the best songs to date. I'm not sure at this point who is playing on it or who will produce. The songs are written and will be reinterpreted by the best I know. We will see how the paint sticks to the wall when it's said and done.

As far as advice, boy I'm not qualified to really answer this but, Do it, it meaning music because you love it, play what you want to play because your heart is in it and behind it, and don't chase trends they end faster than you think. Put time into your instrument(s) and don't let anyone tell you "You Can't".
Jeremy

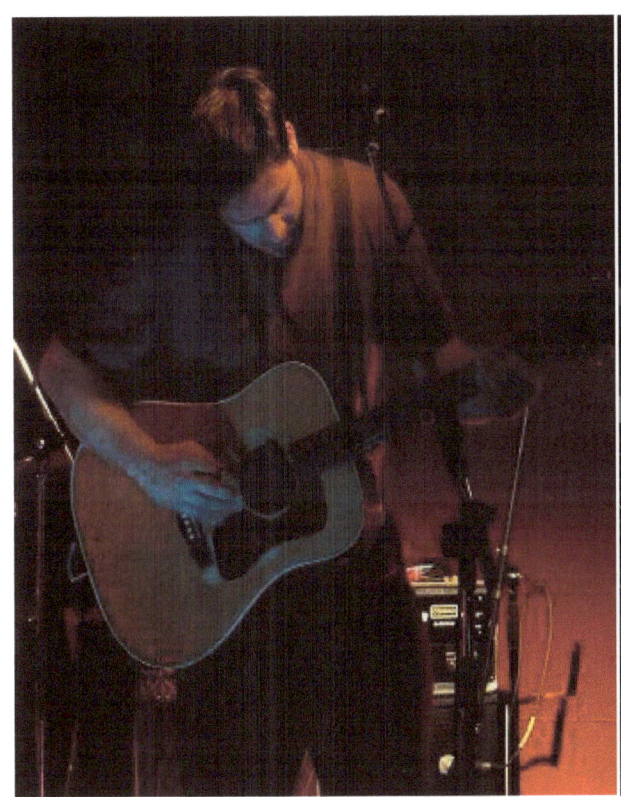 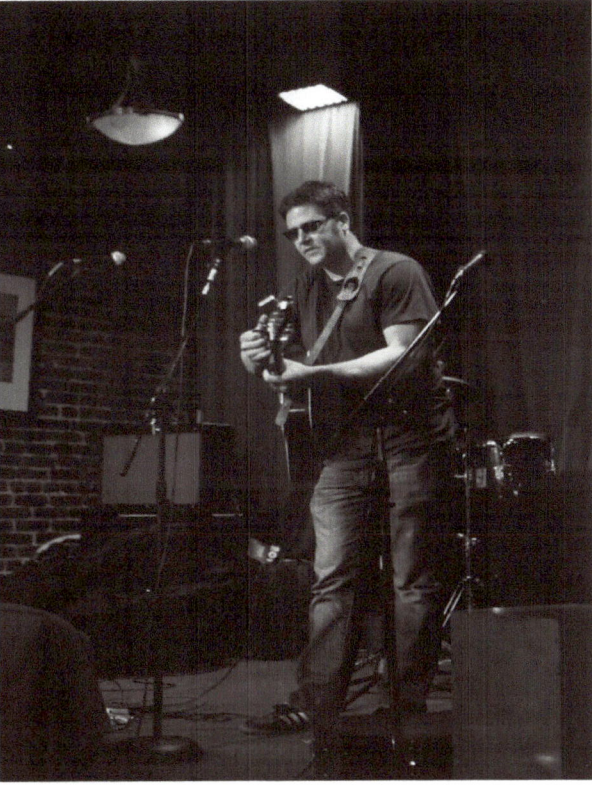

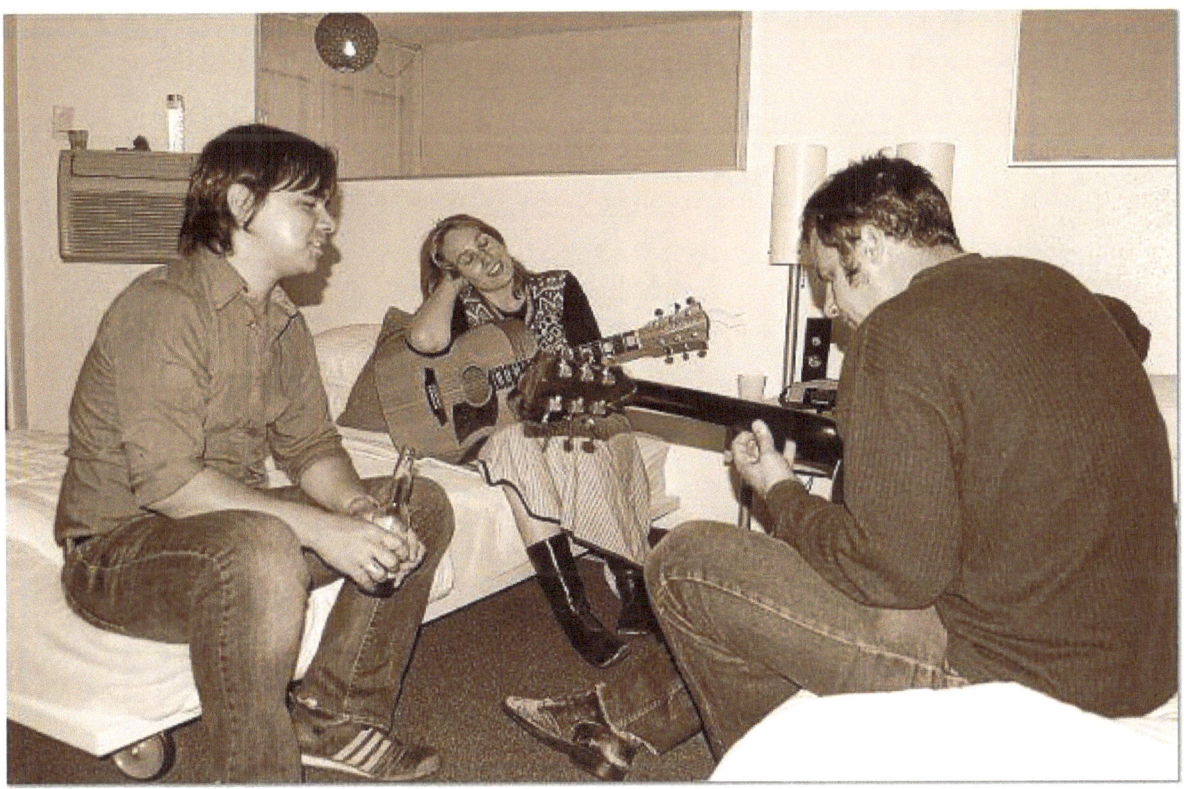

Jeremy Serwer

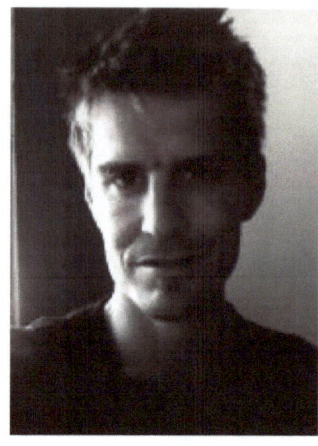

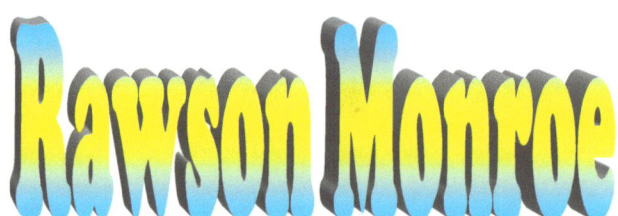

As my time as an artist over the years I have had many successes and failers as an artist and making a living for myself through the expression of art forms. I persued fine arts at a university which was paid for through grants, loans, scholarships and work.

As I attended art classes it built knowledge with hands on criculums that made my days be devoured in creativity. Writing papers on art itself, art history, painting hours on end with other artist ect. molded me into the artist I am today. Outside learning fine arts at a university. I found myself painting murals, teaching art to children for after school programs and putting together art shows at local restaurants, cafes and galleries.

The success as an artist came not just from attending art classes that gave me the tools to make my art into a career that would pay my way through life but putting myself as an artist by promoting my work and getting my name known in the local community is the magic key to being a successful artist. You have to push yourself and If one door closes than find a new avenue that will open up new doors to have your work viewed by the public.

To create a snowball of creativity is the first and hardest part to being an artist trying to get work shown but to keep it rolling into an avalanche is the beautiful struggle as a starving artist. I believe the hardest struggle as an artist is to get the ball going. But one must recognize that the more you build your portfolio the easier it will be to get your work shown and sold.

My advice to other artists is to keep thriving to have excellent work that others enjoy, keep an open mind towards negative criticism and never give up with getting the community around you to view your work and remember art is in the eye of the beholder. If you keep creating and applying that creatvity to the outside world others will notice your ambishion and passion for creativness and others are the ones who make dreams come true by supporting your creativity.

I now am skipping back and forth from Seattle to Berkeley, California and I am pursuing my artistic passions by creating murals in as many places along the globe as I can get a can against a wall and working by my side with youth and people of all ages in his community and surrounding areas for a creative and positive atmosphere that adds value to our everyday lives and keeps a reminding me to never lose the child in us all.

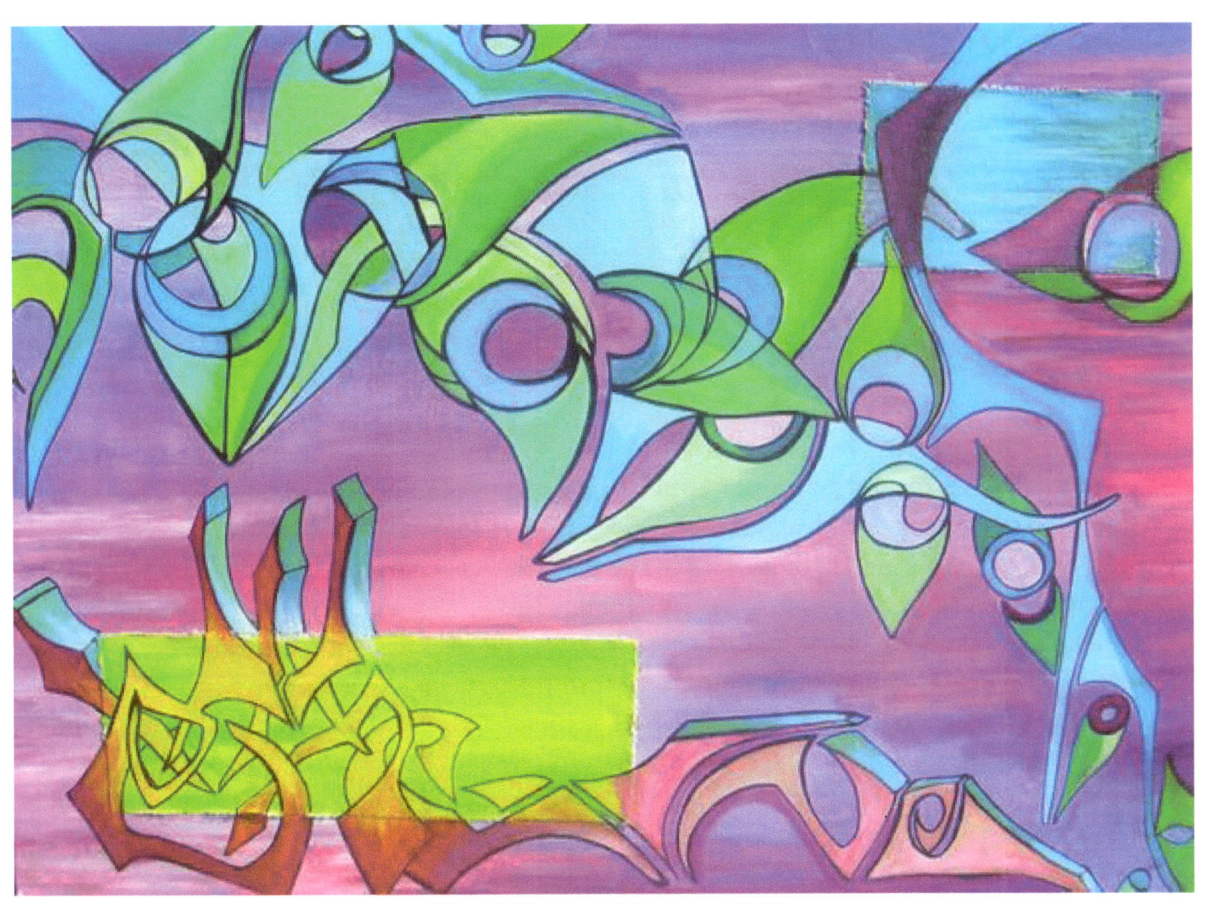
"Crepe Vines" Rawson Monroe ,2009

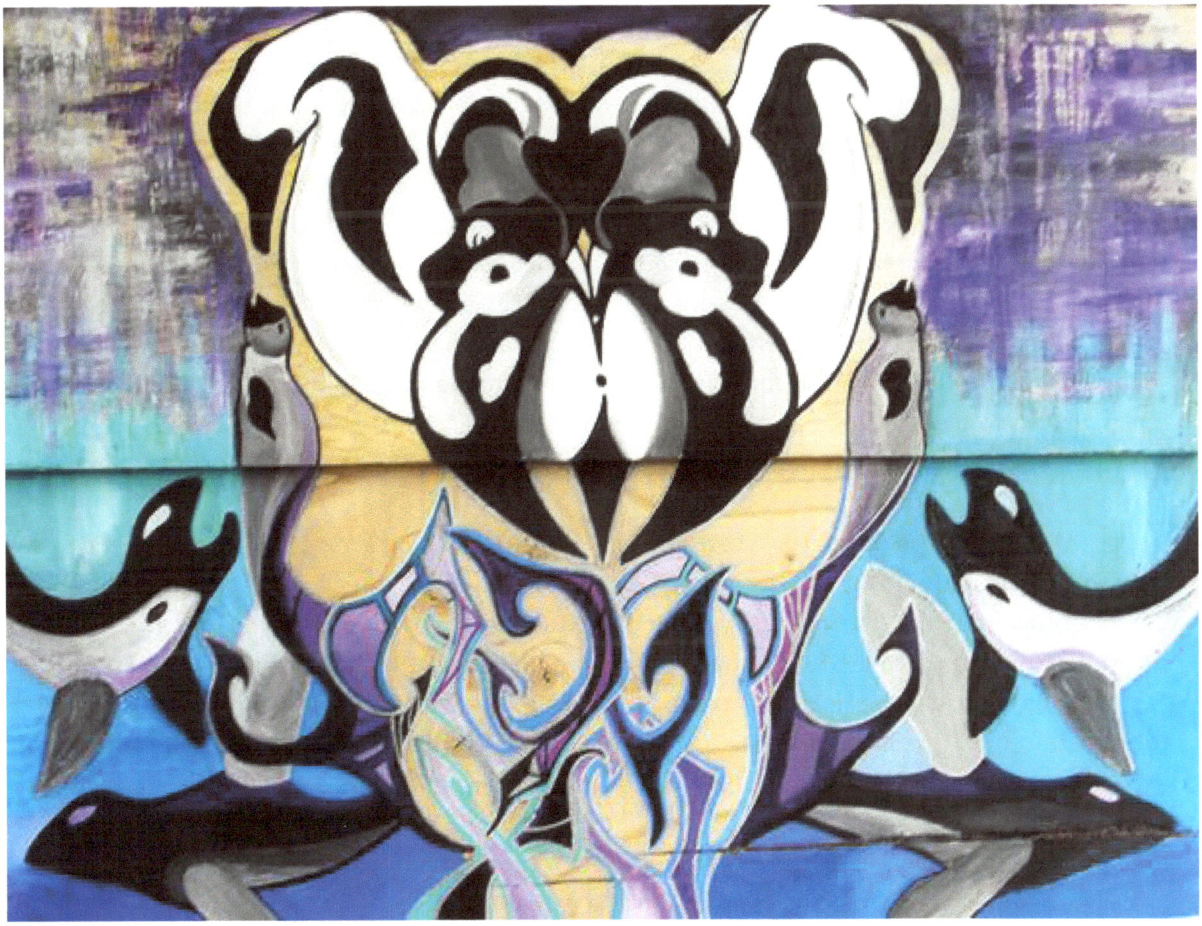

Rawson Monroe

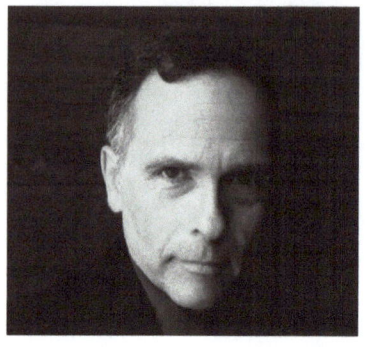

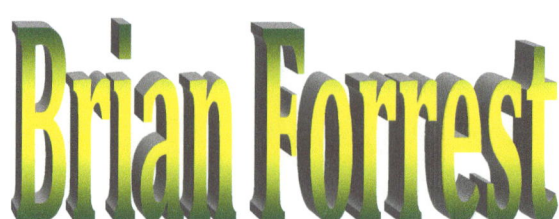

Doing art is a cross between a crap shoot, finding your way out of the woods, and performing a magic act. Each time I begin to paint I feel like I am walking a tightrope—sometimes scary, sometimes exciting, sometimes very quiet, and always, always surprising; leading me where I never expected to go. Doing art makes me lose all sense of time and place and go inside one long moment of creating.

Whenever I feel a painting in my gut, I know this is why I paint. Its colors are the message. I feel them before my mind has a chance to get involved. Color is the most agile and dynamic medium to create joy. And if you can find joy in your art, then you've found something worth holding on to.

I work in many mediums: oil painting, computer graphics, theatre, digital music, film, and video. I studied acting at Columbia Pictures in Los Angeles, digital media in art and design at Bellevue College (receiving degrees in Web Multimedia Authoring and Digital Video Production.) I work in the Seattle, WA area in design/media/fine art. Influenced by past and current colorist painters, my style can hover between realism and abstraction.

My background and training is not at an art school, but in multimedia: film/video/theater/digital. To me a painting is really no different than any other creative work I have done; just the medium has changed—oil paint. I find traditionally trained artists and I speak a different language. They seemed concerned with some nebulous criteria of aesthetic—I prefer to speak in plain language that the average man on the street can resonate with. I believe art must generate a sensation that is strong enough to evoke a meaningful feeling in its viewer.

I was compelled to begin painting while undergoing an intensive Reichian Therapy program. This therapy is very physically demanding, it literally retrains the body to breathe deeper, relax chronic muscle tension, and tolerate a higher energy charge. The need to paint was always inside me, but I had been cut off from this need due to intense negative life experiences. The body-mind reacts to repeated negative experience and builds a shield of control within our musculature and personality. Everyone has experienced repression, but few are aware of the effects on their health. Some continue on, lost, searching for what really matters to them, when the core values they are looking for are cut off due to their own repressive structure. Reichian Therapy loosens this repressive structure allowing our core values break through so we may discover our true needs and desires in life.

My influences in painting are both past and present. I find parallels between the painting styles of the European impressionists, expressionists, and those of contemporary artists in the United States. Of all the American artwork, I am particularly attracted to the San Francisco Bay Area painters. From the color ism of the Society of Six in the 1920's and 1930's to the 1950's and 1960's with the Bay Area Figurative.

In painting, to one side of the spectrum you have representational realism the other end you have total abstraction—I prefer the working in the middle. In doing so, an artist must decide what details to keep, what to leave out, what shape or color to recreate and what to push.—in short, when an artist works in the middle ground he/she must choose and in doing so, their unique approach and style emerges. I feel every one of my paintings is just a self-portrait, just an expression of process of the painting itself: all the emotions and feelings I experienced as I painted it are revealed to the keen observer, it's all there, my secrets are not hidden, but naked to the world.

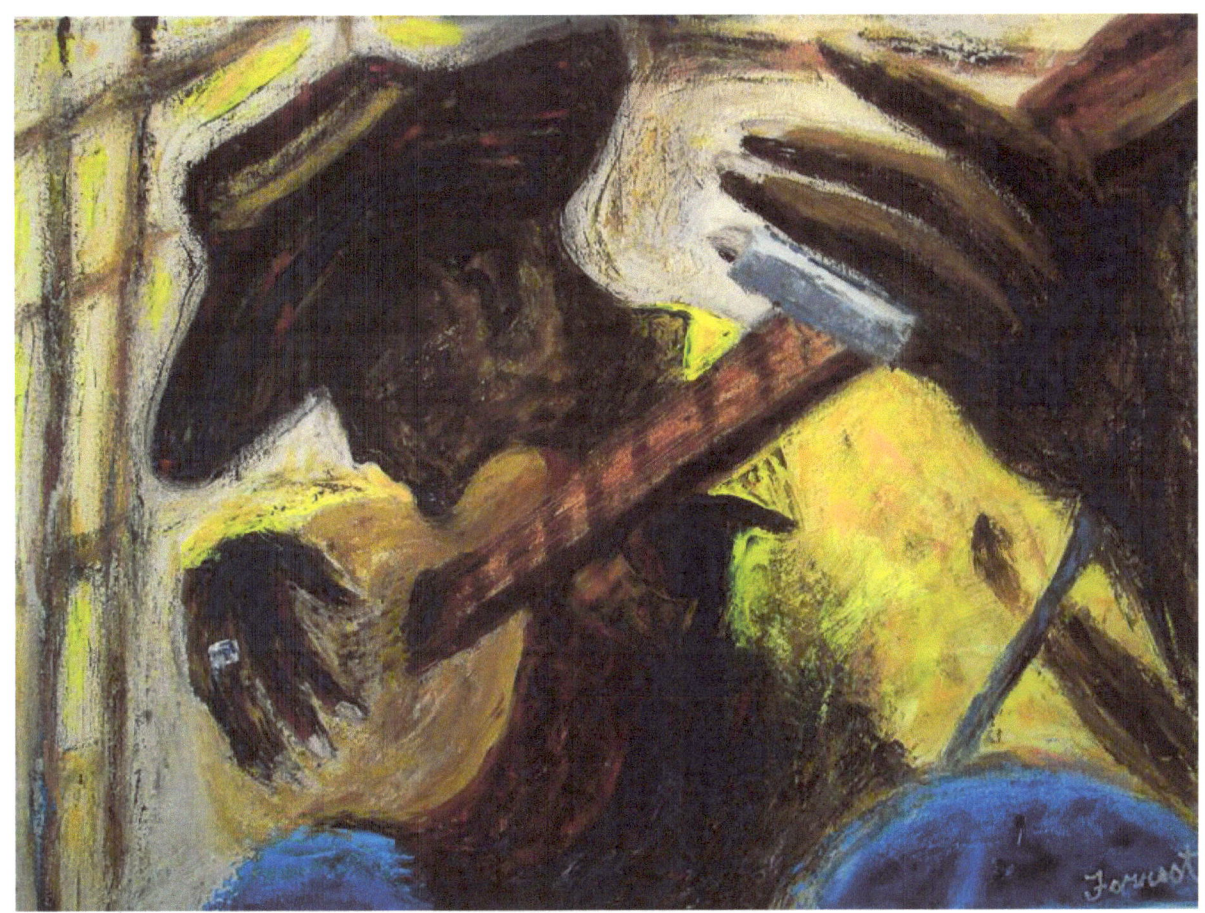

"Bluesman" Brian Forrest

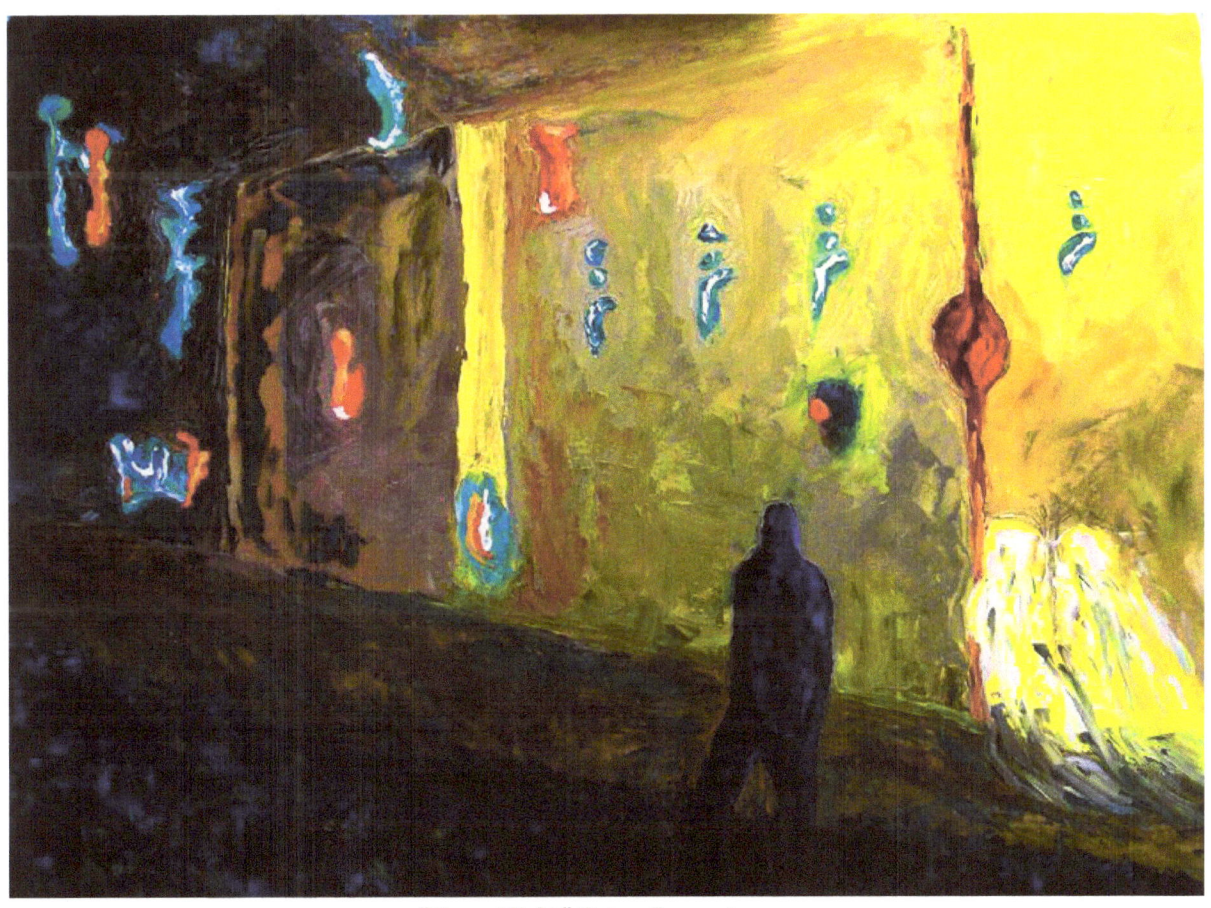

"Neon Night" Brian Forrest

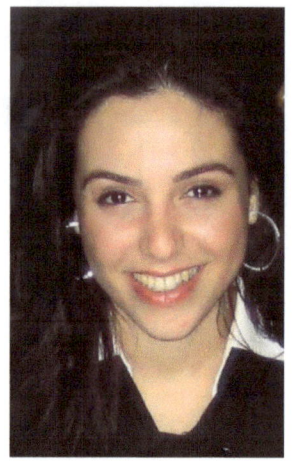

Rana Ghezelayagh

I am a fashion designer today because the seeds of creativity and attention to detail were planted in me at a very young age. I was born and grew up in an artistic family. My father is an architect; my mother was a musician and the folkloric choir singer; my late aunt was a famous national singer; and my uncle was a civil engineer who ultimately turned out to become a painter. My family was always bringing music, art, and nature into my life, and I was constantly involved with my mom's performances or my father's projects. As my mom says, I was always passionate about colors, textiles and creating something new. When I was a little girl, I always wanted to choose my own dress with my matching purse and shoes whenever we went shopping. But, it seemed not only I didn't let my mom pick my clothes, I also wanted to choose for her as well.

Based on the education system in Iran, one has to choose their academic major that will determine one's future career just after middle school (before high school). Students would have only four choices: Mathematics, Science, Literature and Humanities, or Art. My mother always wanted me to work more on my creative talents and choose Art. My father wanted me to use my problem--solving and analytical skills and become either an engineer or a doctor. Based on the circumstances at that time, I thought the best option for my future career was to become an engineer, and so I earned a Bachelor of Science (BS) in Chemical Engineering from Tehran Azad University in 1997.

In July 2006, I immigrated to the United States and decided to make a big career transition and switch to fashion design – my real passion. The realization that this is what I wanted to do hit me at 2:00 a.m. one morning, and I started researching and contacting schools that offered fashion degrees; by 8:00 a.m., I received a call from IADT–Seattle and I was on my way to entering the fashion world. The IADT staff was very nice and encouraging while we were touring through the different departments of school, so I became even more convinced and determined about what I want to do for my next career.

It was not easy to start a complete new major which is not in your native language after being out of school for a long time, along with working near--fulltime as a teller at a commercial bank (to have some income for living and paying for school); and it especially became even more challenging after I moved, helped remodel the new house, and got engaged and planned a wedding. But it all happened with hard work, little sleep, and the guidance and aid of very helpful teachers in school.

After I received my Associate of Applied Science degree in Fashion Design in March of 2009, I started freelance designing for family & friends and made my own wedding gown which I modeled in the 2009 IADT – Seattle "Imagine" Fashion Show. I began work on my first collection during the spring/summer of 2009, and on Dec. 6, 2009 (right after my wedding), I showcased my first fashion show in Kirkland, WA featuring my Para collection of trench coat dresses. Para is a fashion forward statement designed with the trendy, chic, sophisticated, and yet practical businesswoman in mind. The architectural beauty of the ancient city called "Persepolis" in Iran inspires the lines, color and structure of my designs, and their influence can be seen in this collection. Also at the same time as my debut fashion show, my website for my brand "anar Couture" [http://www.anar-couture.com] was launched.

My show was successful in confirming for myself that I was capable of completing an entire collection, creating an online presence, and organizing an event that could show an audience of target consumers what anar Couture is about. The pace of the fashion world is extremely fast, but I am excited for the journey I am embarking. I have the courage and confidence to create a niche for my creative, innovative work.

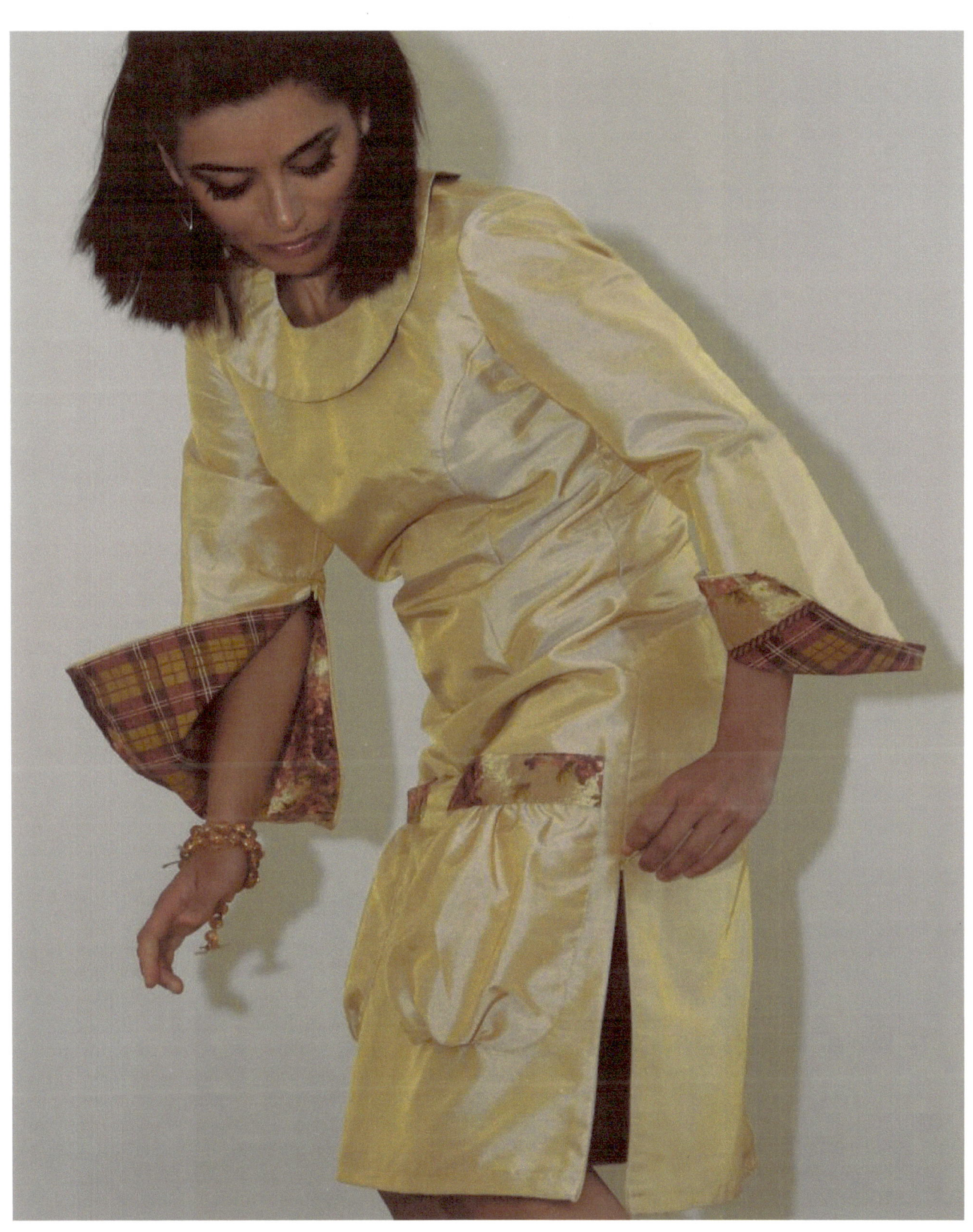

"Para Collection" Rana Ghezaelayah ,2010

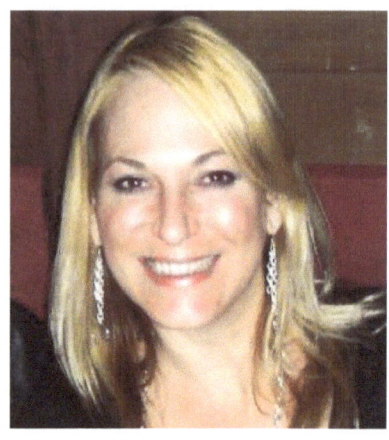

Jenny Gini Prochaska

The only child of a single parent, I had a fairly solitary childhood so drawing became my main source of entertainment. While my mother worked or ran errands I often filled my time alone with art and crafts of any kind. In kindergarten I won a school art contest for a silhouetted yucca plant with a warm sunset. The following year I won a city wide contest for a Christmas poster and had my picture taken with my poster, which appeared in the Las Vegas Review Journal. At age 10, my mother enrolled me in private art lessons on Saturday mornings. I remember hating getting up early and missing the best cartoons, but as soon as I began to paint I'd forget all about everything else. In high school I took every art class I could get into. Though the skill and talent of some of my peers intimidated me at times, being in art class was my favorite part of the day.

Being a Las Vegas native I started college in my hometown at UNLV. After my first year there I found the art department to be disappointing and fled to greener pastures, literally. I moved to California as a young adult. I attended Cabrillo College in Santa Cruz, and later relocated to San Francisco where I graduated from SFSU with a bachelor's in Fine Art. Eventually I returned to my hometown, amazed at the beauty of the desert I'd taken for granted in my youth. I earned a teaching certificate and began teaching art at the middle and high school level. I believe I learned more as a teacher than I ever had as a student. Giving a classroom of individuals an assignment and seeing such a vast array of interpretations inspired me. I continued to produce my own art when I could, but I soon realized teachers don't really have as much time to themselves as I presumed. My commitment to creating my own art was not my top priority at that time; my students were.

I taught for six years and got married in the meantime. My husband was concerned over my growing frustration with overcrowded classes and school politics. He and his family encouraged me to focus fully on my own art and I left my teaching position to pursue a career as an artist. For the last four years I've been actively participating in building a body of work and displaying my art in a variety of venues. Events moved us to the Seattle area a couple of years ago, and I now call Redmond, WA home. The environments that I've had the pleasure of living in play a role in my paintings. My observations of landscapes, as well as people and emotional situations, largely influence my paintings. My inspiration is from beauty in life: up-close and personal portraits with emotional expressions; a window that is opened on the canvas to share a moment capturing a scene into the private life or lives of others; optical illusions that are a surreal make-up of scenery using figures and faces. People, transitory snapshots, and metamorphosis stimulate my creativity and become animated in my mind.

I am grateful to have sold many of my paintings and had the honor of painting several commissions as well. I am fortunate enough to have a partner who carries the financial burdens leaving me able to use my earnings to buy canvases and paint. At times, I'm frustrated when paintings don't sell for a couple of months, or venues choose to eliminate my nude paintings from display. Some locations don't suit my particular type of art at all. It's the marketing of my art that makes being an artist into a job. To just sit and paint, and have my paintings simply sought after by patrons would be heaven. But the truth is I spend more time seeking locations, corresponding with businesses, and hanging and taking down shows then I do actually painting. I continue to paint and display as my full time job, and intend to grow and further thrive as an artist.

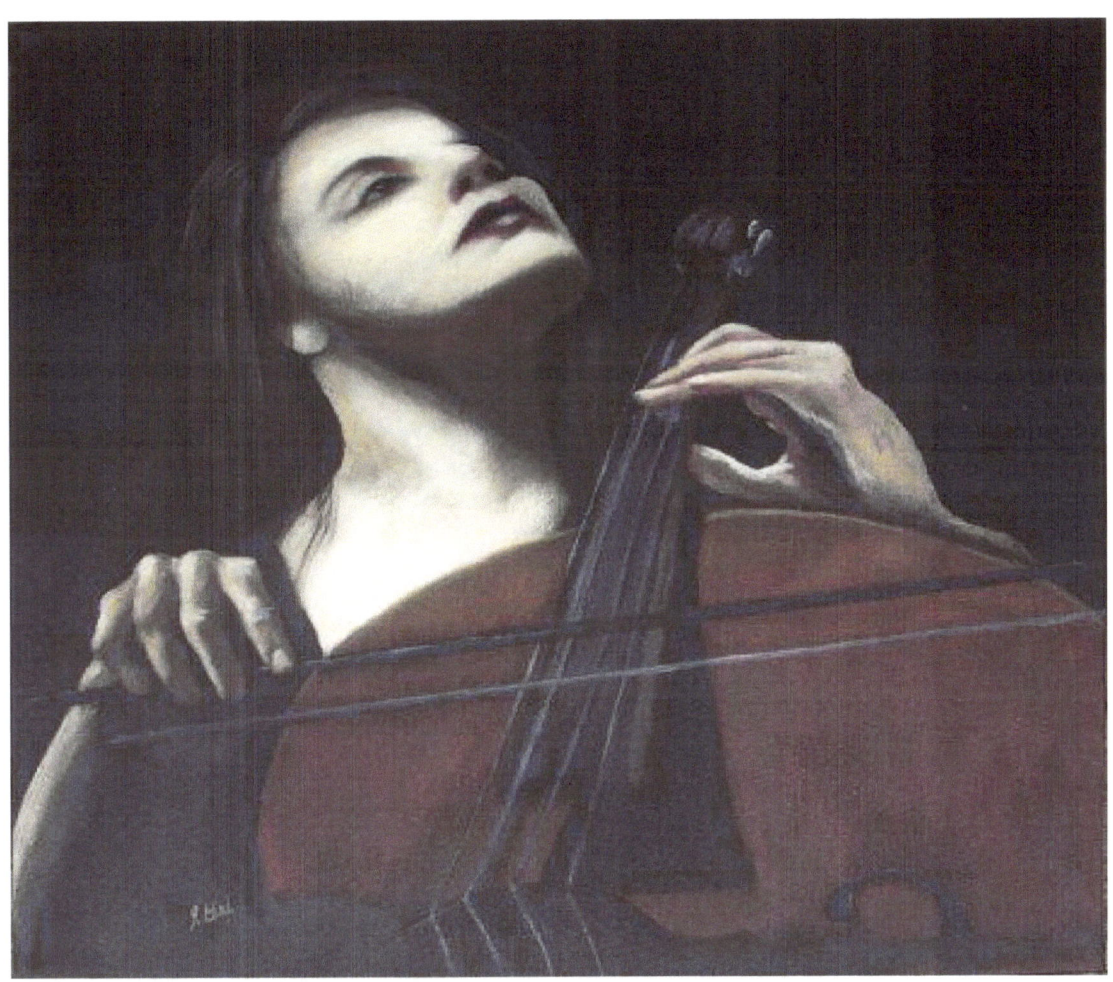

Jenny Gini Prochaska "Cellist" Acrylic 18 x 18

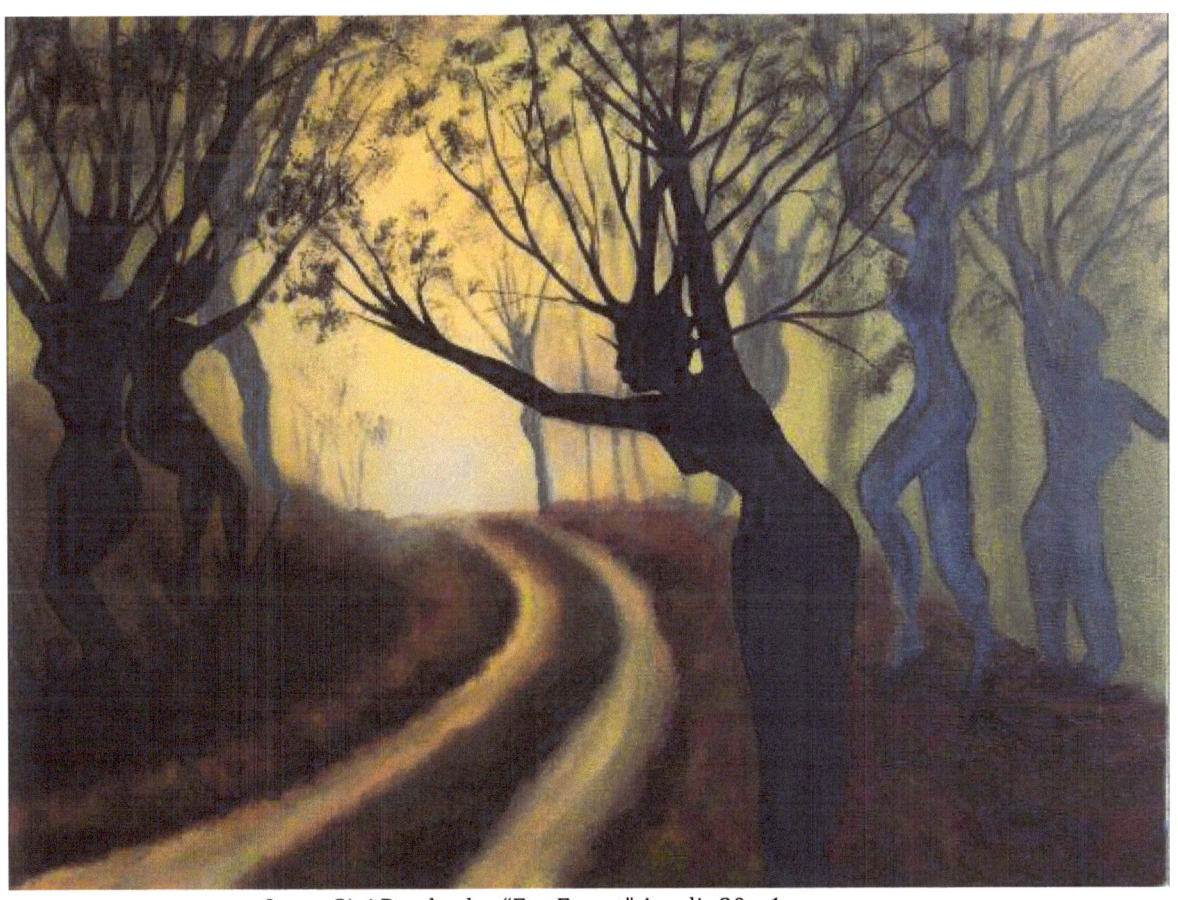

Jenny Gini Prochaska "Fay Forest" Acrylic 20 x 1

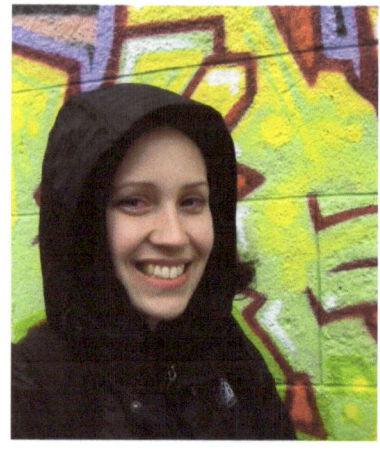

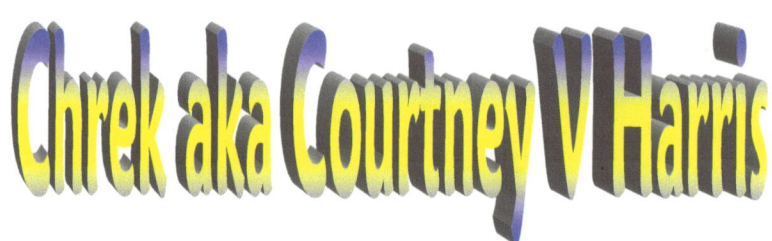

Influences: graffiti, typography, hip-hop, public art, current events, travel, literature, my friends, outsiders...everything
Style: bold, vibrant, high contrast, graphic, playful
Materials: aerosol, acrylics, canvas, wood, metal, Adobe Creative Suite, marker, found objects, silk screen, clothing, photography...anything available

I have been making art in one form or another for as long as I can remember. Craftsmanship is in my blood. My father builds houses, my mother has beautiful calligraphy, and my aunt is renowned for her quilts. Quiet and sensitive, growing up I had difficulty making friends and always felt like an outsider. I spent much of my free time holed up in my room reading, writing, drawing, and dreaming.

I didn't take art seriously until college. I moved from Shoreline to Bellingham to attend Western Washington University, and decided that graphic design might be a practical application for my artistic talent. This was before I knew the joy of routinely peeling open sleep encrusted eyes to the glaring screen of a Mac in the campus lab at 3:00 AM. Besides, I'm not a practical person. But acceptance into the design program also meant that I could enroll in fine arts courses.

While known for its hippies, Bellingham is also home to a thriving hip-hop community. The 4 elements of hip-hop--emceeing, deejaying, break dancing, and graffiti writing--became a huge part of my life. I attended as many local hip-hop shows as I could. As I tackled graphic design projects, my mouse clicked to the rhythm of underground beats streaming through my headphones.

The summer after sophomore year, while visiting a distant city, I was sexually assaulted. The day after, I remember wandering aimlessly through the outskirts of the city, shocked, heartbroken, and painfully alone. I looked up and glimpsed a colorful graffiti mural giving life to otherwise bleak, grey cinderblock walls. I had found my lifeline. Upon returning home, I borrowed a volume of Stylefile from the library, and there was no turning back. I dedicated my free time to practicing my graffiti lettering. Graffiti and hip-hop helped me to maintain sanity amidst depression, stress, and chaos. I could escape into the alternate reality of my sketch book pages. Or adventure out in the night to put up stickers or stencils, or in the day to photograph painted freight trains passing through the city. I eventually gained notoriety from my peers, acceptance and love from the local hip-hop community, and for the first time, a sense that I belonged.

The next summer I made a pilgrimage back to that city. I brought an arsenal of markers and stickers so I could make my mark and fully reclaim my pride. I had the good fortune of randomly meeting the infamous Seventh Letter crew while they were completing a mural, and had Rime tag my notebook. I also ran into Flava Flav at a Burger King.

After graduating from Western, I migrated back to the Seattle area and kept up my artistic momentum for the next year and a half, while working full-time in a print shop. Over time I grew bored with the repetition, ego, consumerism, and lack of innovation I was beginning to feel in graffiti, and bored with life in general. Changes were overdue. I decided to take time to focus on making my life a work of art, rather than allow my art to be an escape from life. I quit my job to travel around Europe (painted a bit overseas, of course!), then delved into things I haven't had much time for these past few years--cooking from scratch, gardening, reading, and hiking. My outlook on life has changed for the better. Sometimes you need to allow room for growth and change in order to get your inspiration back.
From here on out, "Life is my art, and art is my life."

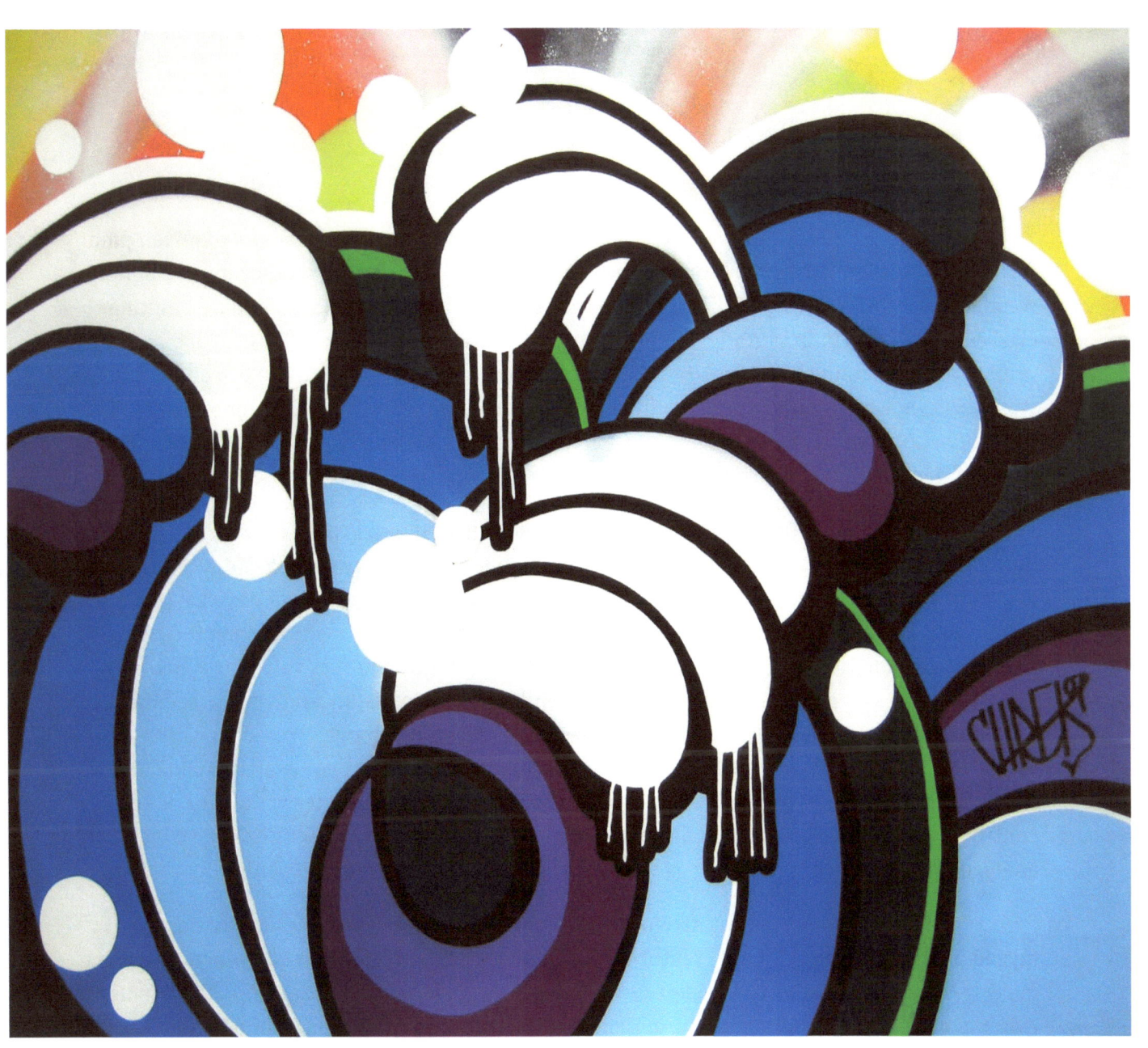

"Washd". Chrek Aerosol, acrylic, and ink on canvas, 2008

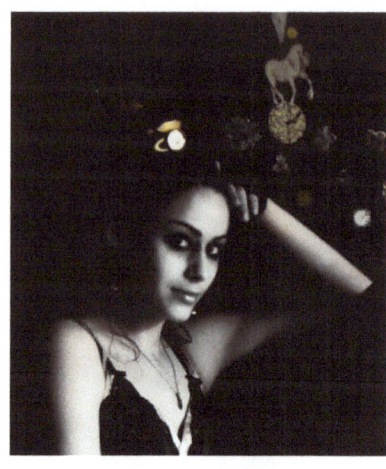

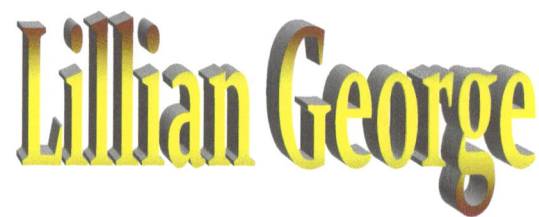

My greatest joy is the psychotic bliss of transforming angst into smears of mixed paint on a once static white canvas. I torture the canvas out of necessity for art therapy, though it wasn't always this way. My mother, a folk artist, began taking me to pastel and oil painting classes when I was in first grade. I immediately fell in love with the messiness of art. I remember oil painting in a room with 20-25 seasoned artists. I could mix colors and apply washes as well as my adult peers by third grade. At age 10 I won Grand Champion at the Okanogan County Fair. I was the youngest artist in my age category. This achievement fueled my confidence as a young artist.

On April 21, 2000 change swept through like a gust of wind when my sister and I came home to an empty house. I can not disclose what happened that day except that it was everything dreadful that you would not wish upon your worst enemy. That day changed who I am. I utilized my hurt as a form of armor so nothing could damage me more than the pain I had already endured. I excelled in academics graduating high school as valedictorian of my class. My successes came at the cost of close friends who were distanced by my arrogant outward appearance. After high school I moved to Western Washington to further my education. I earned a Bachelor Degree in Fine Arts with a Studio Art concentration in Oil Painting. Students didn't understand my artwork in college critiques. It was said to be too controversial, too dark, too much like a 13 year old girl starved for attention. They tried to analyze the meaning of my paintings without knowing the context of its history.

The past transformed my artwork into what it is today. I have since found peace with myself and paint strangely cute creatures into hazy abstract environments. My process of art making begins by painting the background of the canvas. Here I vent frustrations by means of ripping into paint with a pallet knife and mixing in dirt or found objects. While the oil paint dries I draw creatures and oddities on squares of cardstock. I then watercolor and carve them out with an exacto knife. Scrapbooking papers and drawn cutouts are arranged on the painted surface. This creates a flat yet three dimensional appearance which becomes more apparent to the viewer as they walk closer.

I am inspired by my surroundings. I observe peoples habits, take humorous quotes from my significant other, and capture colors as the seasons change. My paintings tell stories. They are the stories of who I am and what I have experienced in this lifetime. I cannot lie for my art will always expose the truth.

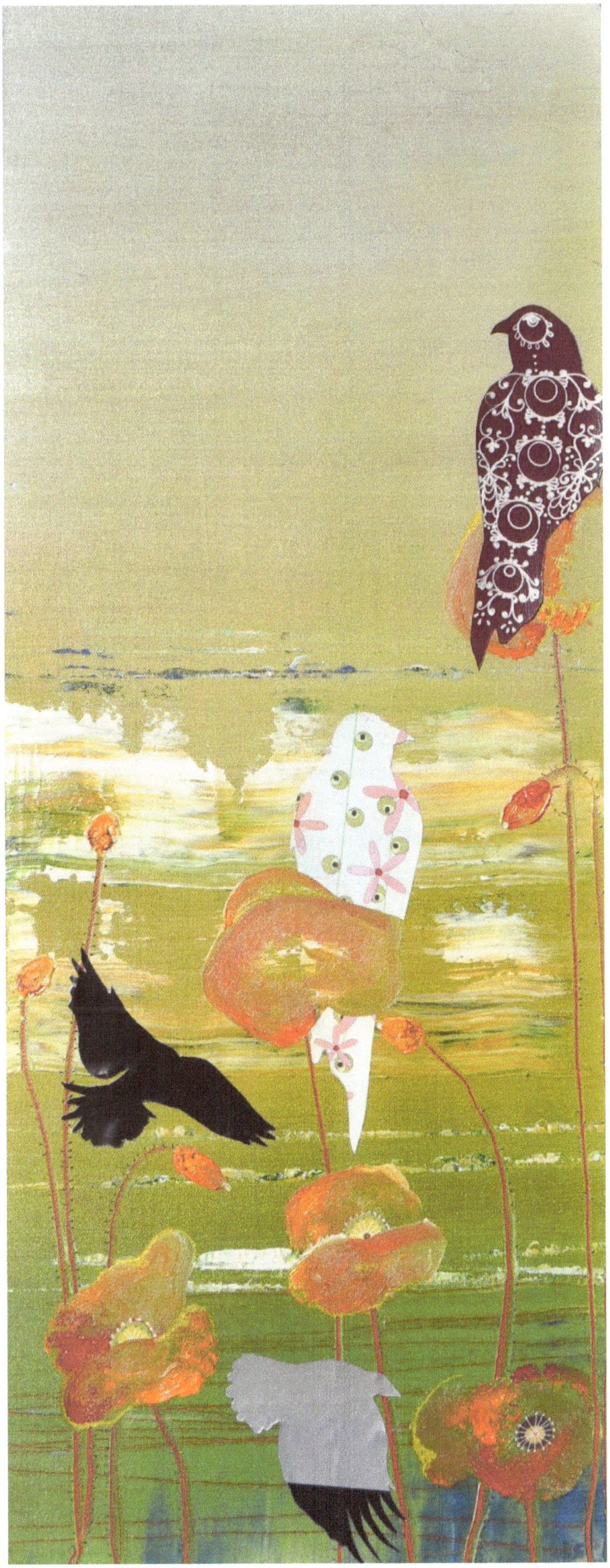

"A Change of Season." Lillyan George, 12"x30" 2010

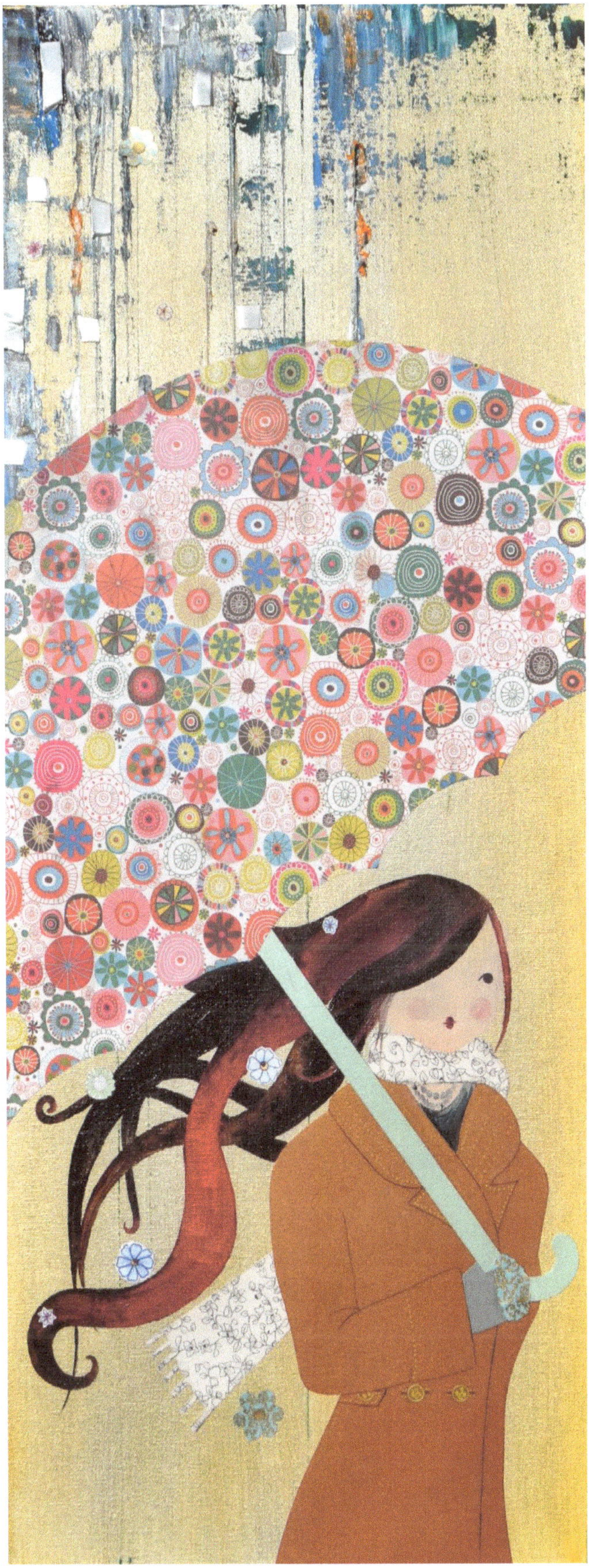

"Umbrella Armor"   12"x30" 2010

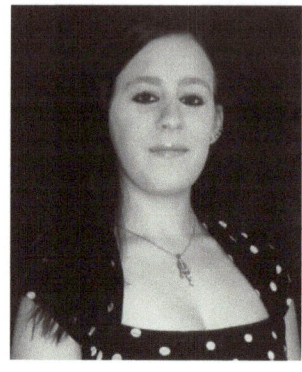

Amanda Hager

Art runs through my veins like blood; everywhere I turn I see, breathe and eat art. I have aspired to be an artist since I was seven. I have been drawing my whole life and have developed many other talents along the way, which I no doubt inherited from my biological father. However, I strongly believe it is because of my family, friends and everyone else in my life who appreciated my artwork that I'm the artist I am today. I have come to realize over the years that when people tell me they like my artwork they aren't saying it just to be nice, they actually like it! My first realization came about with my drawing I titled "Art Supplies", a piece I was truly proud of. I showed it to my mom and stepdad Gary. They loved it, especially my stepdad Gary, who liked it so much that he asked me if he could have it. I gave it to him which was huge because I never let anyone have my artwork because I didn't think it was worth having. This experience made me realize I had a raw untrained talent that people really liked.

Over the past year I have become quite the entrepreneur. I draw, paint, design logos, layouts, clothes, jewelry, tattoos, and ad's, write children's books, do visual merchandising, photography, and want to someday do voice over work as well. I used to dream that one day, while walking down the street, of seeing a logo I designed or a mural I painted on the side of a building. Of walking into a restaurant and seeing a photo I took or drawing/painting I made hanging on the wall. To turn around and see someone wearing the clothes I designed or the jewelry I made. To one day know I made people happy with my gifts.

Today at twenty two years old those dreams are slowly coming true. I currently draw pictures on the windows of a local store and design layouts for their products. Yeah it's not a picture or painting hanging in a restaurant, clothes or jewelry on someone's body, or my own voice on TV, but my artwork is out there for people to see and appreciate! I'm making it! Every day I search for artist jobs on the internet; I haven't been booked for any but know one day I will.

I love to try new things with my art and use all sorts of mediums. My favorite is pencil because I can get great detail work done with it. But I also love to use charcoal to get bigger faster pieces done. I enjoy using water color, acrylic, tempera and oil paint. I have just started using oil paint and cannot put it down. Another favorite of mine is digital art work; I enjoy making collages using Illustrator and Photoshop cs3. I am constantly snapping photos and literally am running out of space for all of them. I want to continue to learn new mediums, and I hope to develop new artist concepts, and to maybe even develop a new genre of art one day.

Not many people want to hear advice from someone who would still be considered a struggling artist but I'm slowly working my way up and have much to offer. Here are my words of wisdom. Keep trying and when you fail try again and again. Many of us struggle and all we see is our goals that we are not achieving. But what we don't see is that this all struggling to make it is a gift. It not only makes us better at what we love but it makes us a better stronger person. We learn the do's and don'ts of life, find out who our true friends are, get tons of practice at what we love, and we even find out who we truly are. It's a long path for some to reach their dreams, an artist life if a tough life and every "artist is their own worst critic". For me the struggle is what it's all about and I'm slowly becoming my biggest fan.

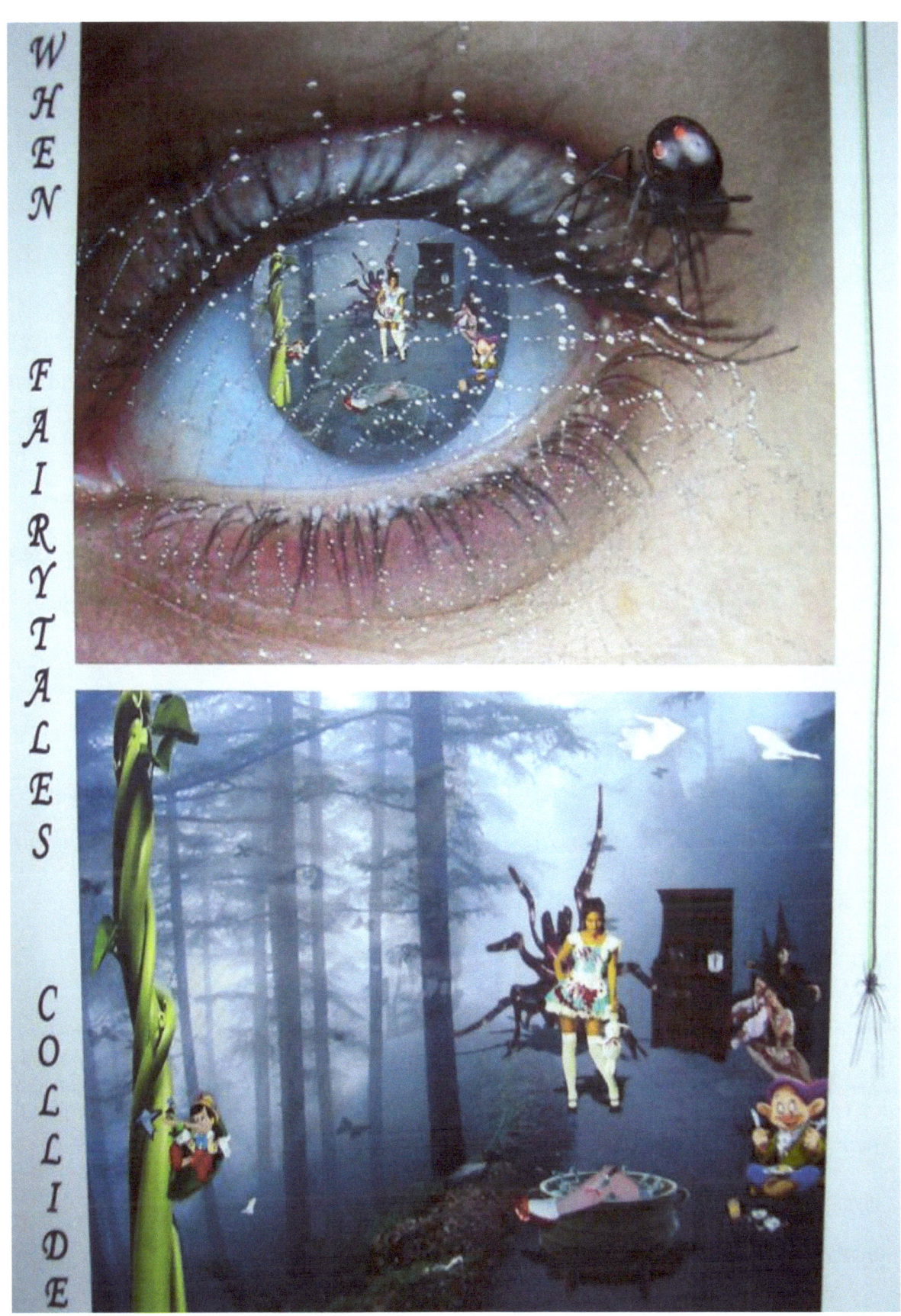

"When Fairy Tales collide" Amanda Hager, digital photos 2008

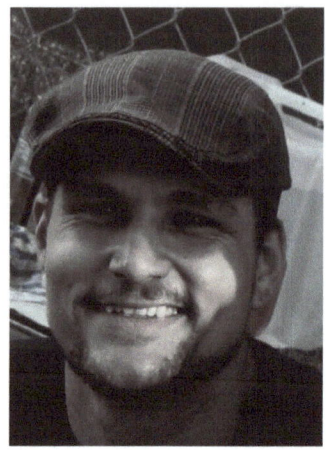

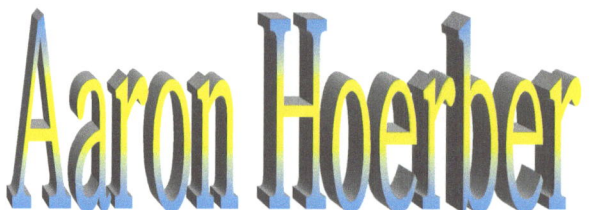

It seems as if I have been creating art since I was a child. I have an encouraging and artistic family that spent their holidays drawing and making clay sculptures. The matriarch of my family was my grandmother who was an art teacher and an avid painter. As I got older my grandmother became a mentor, giving me fine art lessons as early as middle school. Much of what my grandmother taught would take years for me to fully appreciate but this helped form a naturalistic drawing style from early on.

Drawing became an outlet for me to excel, being mediocre at sports or school work I could always take pride in my art. Even though the world of art seemed illusive and unattainable I went forward with studying fine arts in college. Through upper education I sought a wide variety of materials and techniques including glass blowing, bronze and glass casting, ceramics, printmaking, figure drawing, painting and sculpture.

After graduating from California State University Chico with a Bachelor's degree in Fine Arts, I used art for self discovery and commentary. Art gave me a vehicle to express myself and my political opinions in a manner that does not require an answer to my own questions. Visual art gives me the freedom of putting something forth to the public, letting the viewer bring their own interpretation and opinions. This creates an unspoken dialog with the artist and the viewer making the transference of information personal and unique with every encounter.

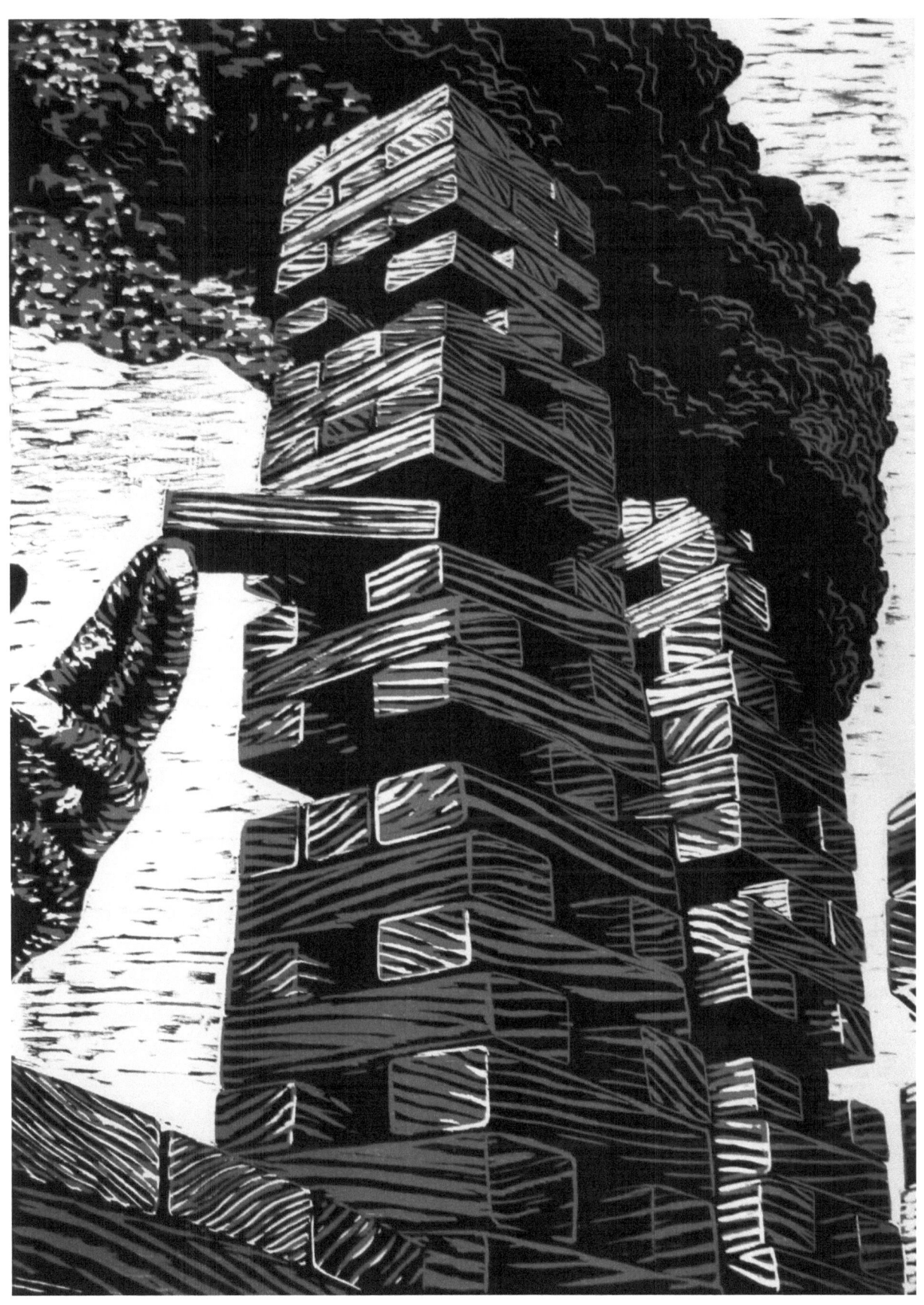

"War Games" Aaron Hoerber, Woodcut, 2008.

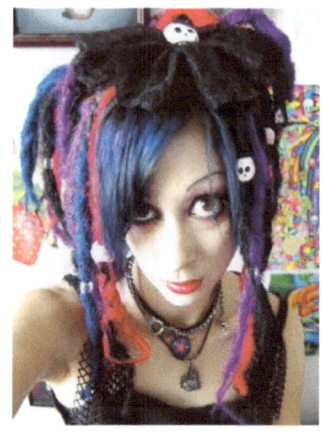

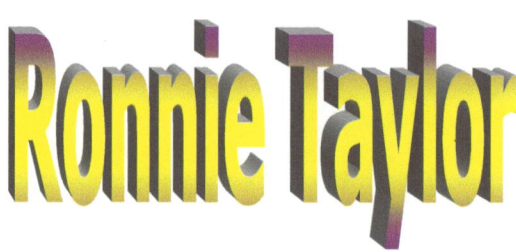

From the time I learned to pick up a crayon, I knew I was destined to be an artist. It was the most obvious talent I had from the start. I scribbled with glittery crayons, brushed wet paint onto paper and canvas, and made collages out of various sparkling ribbons, sequins, and other materials. One quality that has stuck with me is the use of bright colors. This aspect will continue to appear abundantly in my work as my art evolves.

Friends, family, and teachers responded positively to my work. I won many awards for art in elementary, middle, and high school. By senior year, I was awarded the Most Outstanding Art Student. I didn't do much contemporary-style work, because it did not interest me at the time. I stuck with mostly realism and Japanimation/manga. I even applied to art school at Virginia Commonwealth University, excited to strengthen my skills and learn even new things about art. I felt like a star in my school—an art star of sorts. I felt like I was going to succeed in college.

I arrived to college, ready to learn new knowledge and skills. I was ready to make connections and friends with fellow artists and art students. But the first day of art school was a big slap in the face. Suddenly, I found myself to be sitting around 500 other art stars. My work was scoffed at—Who in their right mind would actually think that is *art*? That is not art. These sneers all around me pierced right through whatever confidence I initially had. One professor even suggested that I switch my major to business or something non-art related! Okay, so they didn't like what I do. I just wanted to know why. I felt like I had to twist my art and ideas around so much in order to please my teachers and classmates, that it wasn't "Ronnie art" anymore—it was *their* art now. I did what *they* wanted, just so I could get good grades. In other words, I really had to sell out to make others happy. But, on the side, I still continued with my art the way I wanted to. I put in so much effort into what I did, and each gallery still rejected me. Finally, after two years of applying, I got accepted into Artemis Gallery, which would accept anyone who has been rejected before. It was a start. After more applying to numerous other galleries and contests (and being rejected each time), I finally landed myself into a well-known gallery. Success!

My friends, family, and the professors on my side encouraged me to keep going. I continued to work hard on my art, dodging insults and smug attitudes towards my work. My hard work and dedication paid off—I graduated Magna Cum Laude Honors in four years.

One personal quality that has always stuck with me is stubbornness. Never give up what you love. Going to college has showed me what it's like in the art world, and while it wasn't pleasant at the time, it really has prepared me. Not everyone is going to like your art. Even fewer artists will like it, and will tell you to quit. But you cannot let that stop you. What would worrying change anyway? Do what you feel. Do what you love, and love what you do. I continue to make my own art, with my own style. I let my art evolve on its own, this time without others trying to make it theirs. And by doing so, the end result is so much more satisfying and rewarding. My main purpose is to inspire others. One of the most amazing that has happened was when someone came up to me and confessed how she related so well to a personal painting of mine. She confided how my art made her feel that she was not alone. The fact that my work can reach out to others mattered more than worrying about making straight A's or money. And speaking of money, I will admit that I cannot survive off selling my work alone, so I have a day job. But I refuse to believe the stigma that a day job defines your identity. I identify myself as an artist, not whatever my day job is. I use my job only as a means to support myself. You can see my identity and personality shine through my art. It's one of the ways I can just be myself and not worry about others think.

Finally, all I can say is to be yourself, and to never, ever give up what you love. Doing so is a form of "suicide." Your art is what you are known and appreciated for. Maybe you will have to tweak things here and there for others at times. But in the end, all that matters is your own happiness and satisfaction.

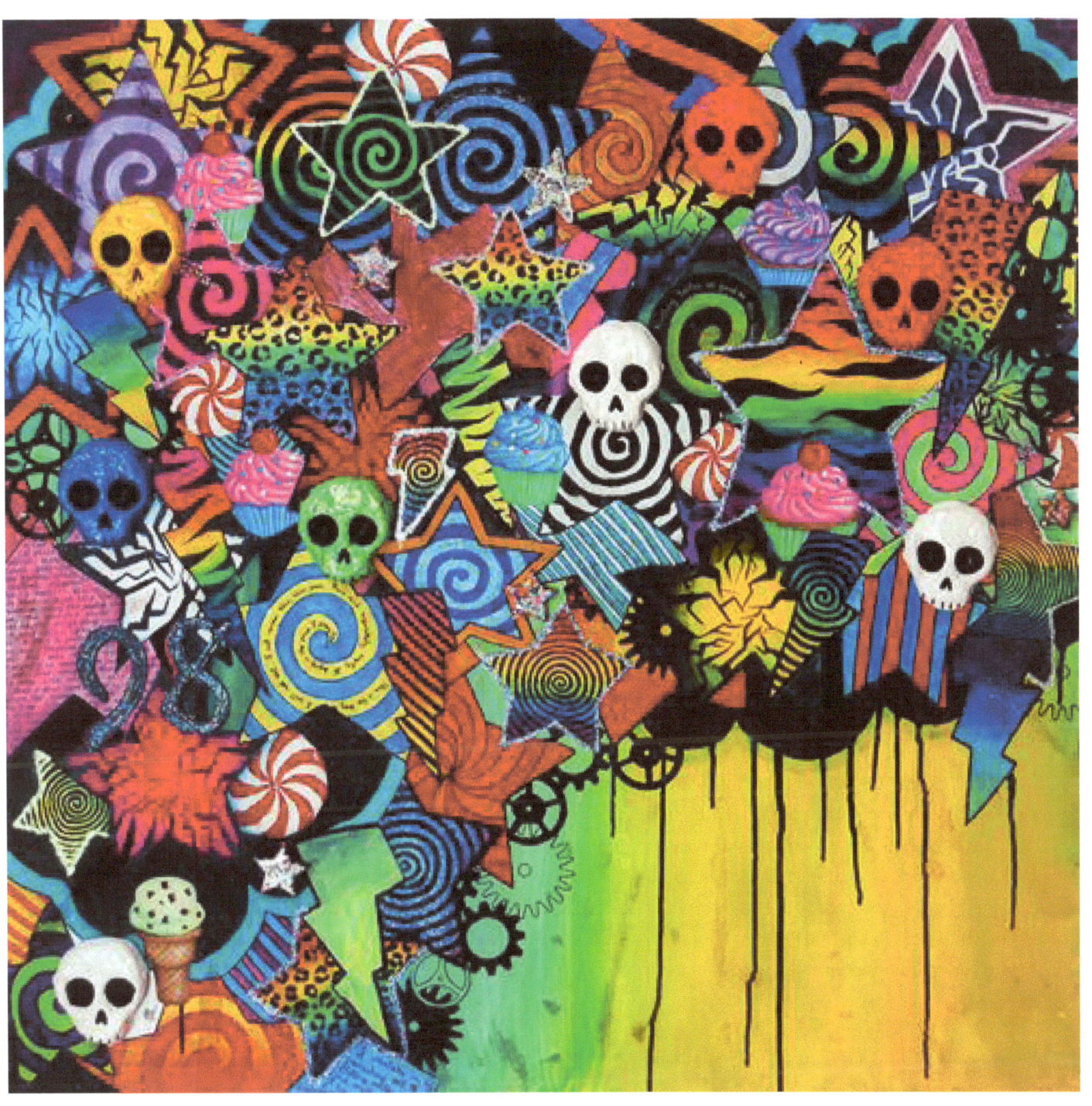

"Consumed: Anorexia and the Endless Neurotic Storm," Ronnie Taylor, Mixed media, 36x36 inches, 2010

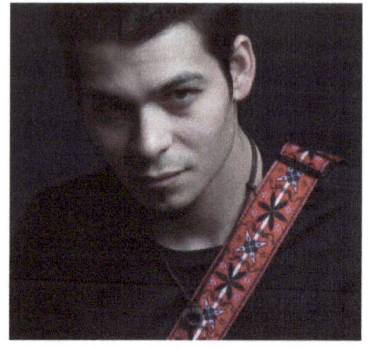

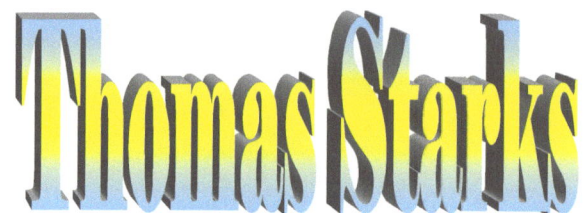

I began writing poetry as soon as I could pick up a pencil at about age 6. Born overseas in the Far East as a result of being a military brat, my family transferred shortly thereafter to San Diego, Ca, the mythical West Coast. Mygreat grandfather was a vaudevillian on the Mississippi River showboat and performed with such greats as "Kid Ory," "Jelly Roll" Martin, Buddy Christian and Tony Jackson. Also rumored in family discussions were performances with then unknowns, Louis Armstrong and child performer, Buster Keaton.

My grandfather never performed publicly, but had mastered the acoustic guitar and played at many family functions. As an amateur poet, I took queues, watched, read, and I listened to the broadcasts and newspaper articles his father produced. By the time I reached adolescence, my father moved the family to Fresno, CA. It was there, at the age of thirteen that I picked up an old, beat-up Washburn guitar and sparked an imperative relationship with music and lyrics. Although I experimented with many instruments, the guitar became my instrument of choice-an inevitable partner. My passion for music ignited and at fifteen, I was sneaking out of my house at night, finding solace at the local music clubs in Fresno.

My passion led to various garage bands, where he played rhythm guitar and vocals, and in time started writing my own songs. After several years of playing in a variety of bands, my experience finally gave the necessary foundation for my songwriting. When I know that life has brought me to a point that mere words cannot describe, music brings me home. I released "Burn the Attic", now on iTunes. "Burn The Attic" seeks to appreciate the history .I have forged and share it on a deeper level. In the hallowed halls of Orbit Audio in historic Pioneer Square, Producer Joe Reineke and I forged into the deep hours of the night to bring about a full array of sound and journey.

In 2007 I recorded my first album "Songs from the Bus Stop" at Elliott Bay Studios. Recently, I had the opportunity to play a few benefit concerts, at the Triple Door and The Tractor where I was on the ticket with Michael Shrieve, the original drummer for Santana. For me, benefit concerts are an important achievement – allowing me to share my passion to help others.

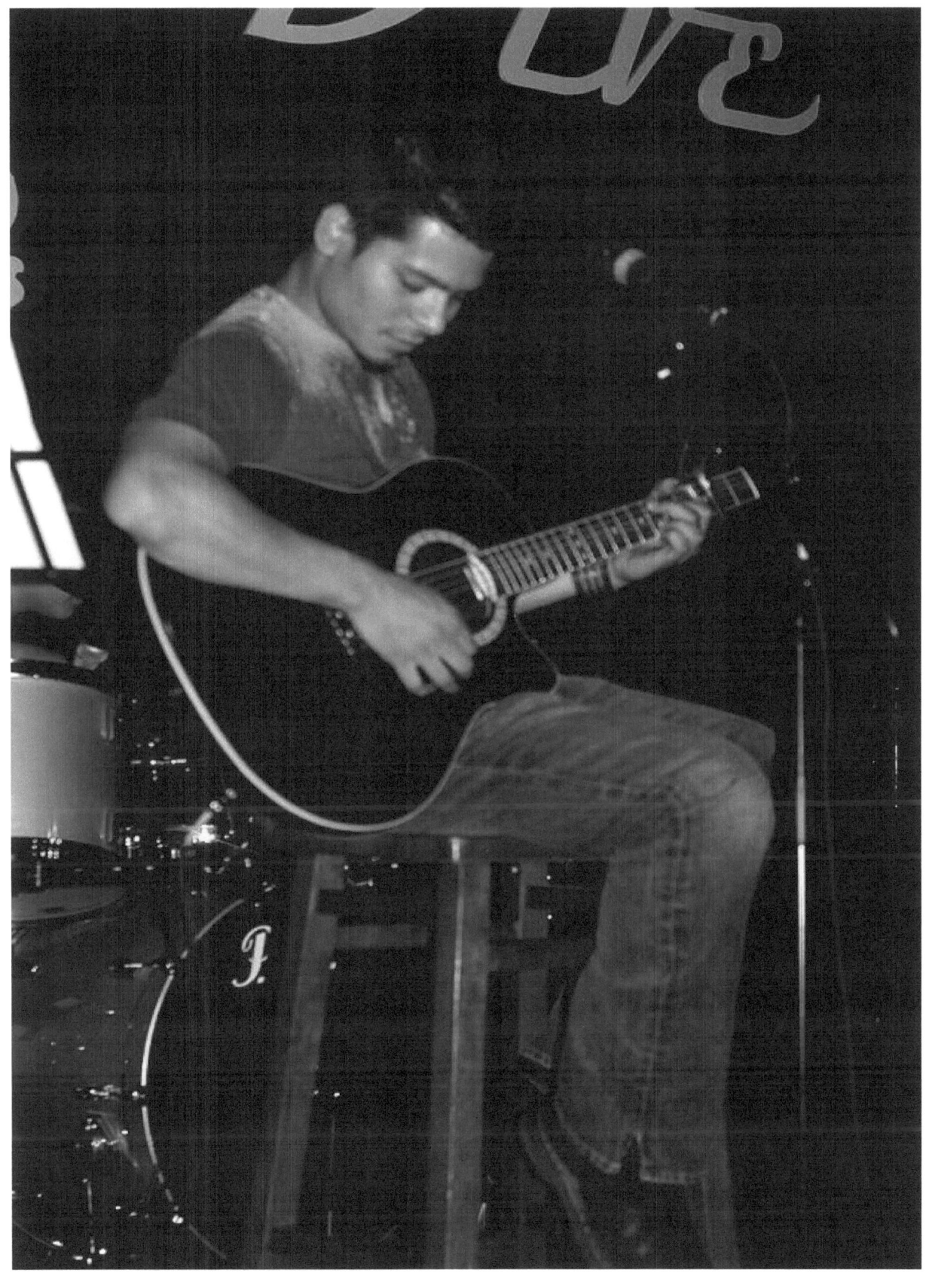

Thomas Starks

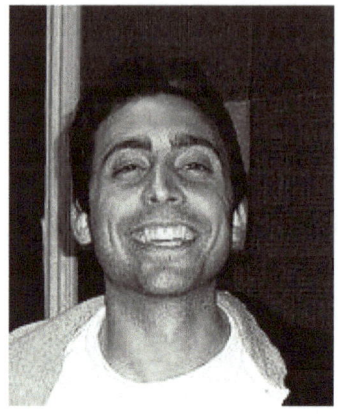

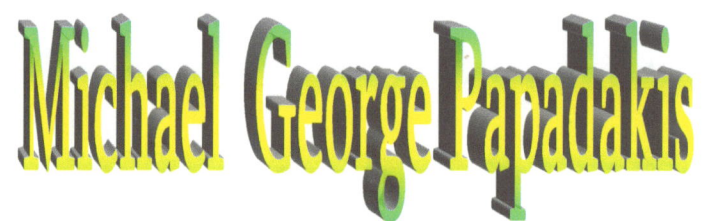

Born: December 22nd, 1986 in Orange County, California

Graduated from San Francisco State University: BA-Fine Arts [Painting]

You'd think that an individual such as myself, one who spends thousands of hours obsessing about a single image, sound, or point, would like to be described as a painter, musician, or sculpture, not exactly. I am a mathematician who doesn't have the attention span to solve complex problems, I am a writer who doesn't like to read, and I am a multi-linguist who learns an accent before learning a language.

I am a composer who can't interpret written music, though I can play various instruments in a non-professional manner and make any audience believe that I know what I'm doing. I'm a filmmaker with no camera, no scripts and no production crew. I am a photographer who doesn't watermark his images because I don't believe in creative licensing, to be specific, I don't believe in taking credit for Mother Nature's organic symmetry. I am a painter who doesn't like to sketch, and uses photographic references as a means to build off of, not to duplicate.

From the looks of my recent sculptures, you'd almost believe I have been working with clay for years, when in fact, it's been less than one. I believe everything is a variation of something else and also believe that if one is good at painting, than he or she should be equally as capable in sculpting, music, etc.

Music is a variant of physics, drawing is a variant of writing, and art is variant of religion. Without the visual, iconic representation of lords or gods, religious authority doesn't have the same strength. If it weren't for the painters and sculptures who turned these beliefs into tangible pagan symbols, we'd have all have a different opinions of what Jesus or Zeus should look like.

I've only begun to respect my hand eye coordination in art & music as a necessary step that will allow my curiosity to expand into the fields of science and mathematics in an attempt to learn the boundaries of my imagination. <u>You have to learn the rules in order to break them</u>. What am I going to do next?

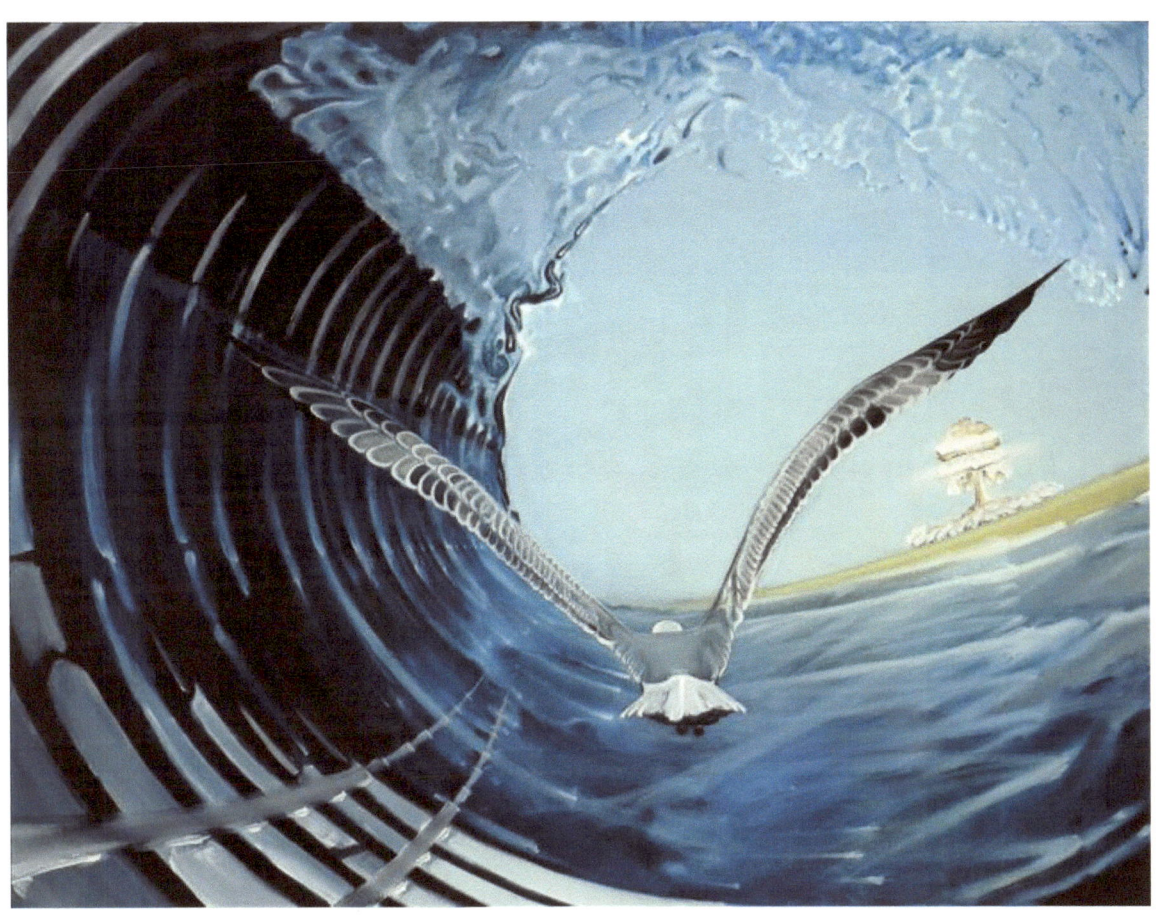

"Distraction" Michael Papadakis, Oils on Canvas-2005

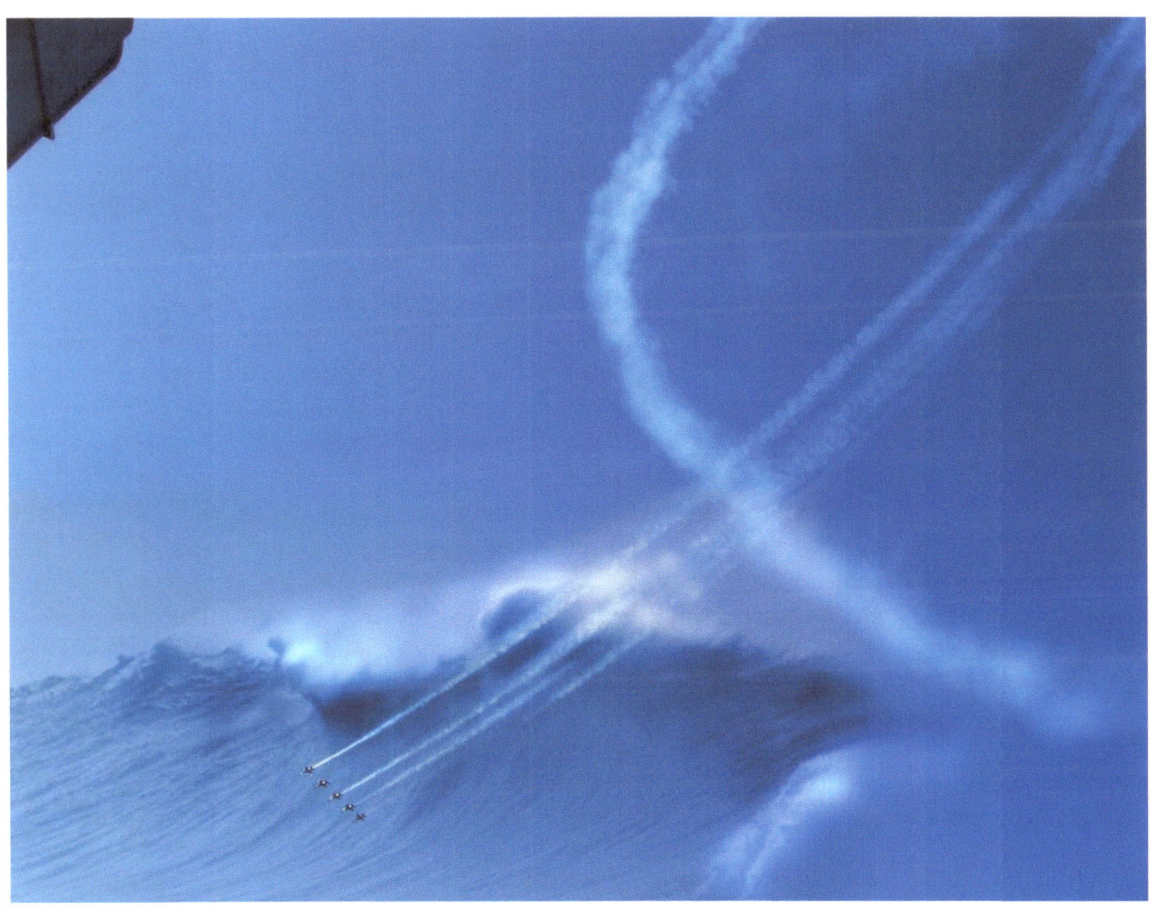

"Trust" Digital Art-2010

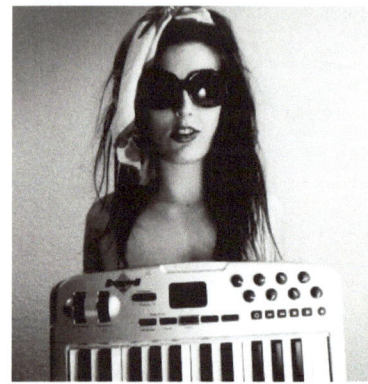

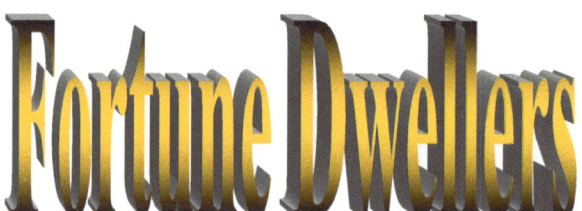

Fortune Dwellers is an original pop/rock/jazz/soul/alternative band based out of Seattle, Washington. Their songs incorporate a wide variety of musical styles but always maintain their pop sensibility.

The music of Fortune Dwellers is driven by the songwriting of Katelyn Berreth. She is the singer and front lady for the band. She has been writing songs since early childhood and her commitment to the art of songwriting has stayed strong throughout her life.

She began playing original music with Martin Celt, the bass player for Fortune Dwellers, in high school. They both wanted to form a band but with college right around the corner they had a hard time finding committed band members. They decided to stick with the name "Katelyn Berreth" until further fortune.

In September of 2006 Katelyn moved from Seattle to Boston in order to pursue her studies at Berklee College of Music. She attended Berklee as a vocal principle and songwriting major.

Katelyn spent her last five quarters of college at The Evergreen State College. Through Evergreen she did an independent contract in order to receive sixteen credits for writing, recording and producing Fortune Dwellers' debut album, *Schizophonic*, during the summer quarter of 2010.

Of course Katelyn and Martin were major contributors to the album, but who were the other musicians on *Schizophonic*? The connections Katelyn made at Berklee ended up paying off on this record. Chris Rude majored in music production and engineering at Berklee, traveled from his home in Los Angeles to engineer, produce and play several instruments on *Schizophonic*. Ehssan Karimi played drums and hang on the album, was home from Berklee for the summer. Evan Anderson, another Seattleite from Berklee, took a few days off from his touring band in Europe in order to record a song that he and Katelyn had written together in Italy. While Katelyn, Evan and Ehssan were all born and raised in the Seattle area, Katelyn didn't meet either of them until they were all at Berklee. There are also some specialty musicians featured on the record. These people include Andrew Joslyn, Phil Peterson, Brennan Carter, Scott MacPherson, Colin Pulkrabek, Andrew Miller, and Ian Sheridan.

Brennan Carter and Scott MacPherson joined the Fortune Dwellers live band shortly after tracking horns on *Yes!* Through the dynamic duo, Fortune Dwellers were introduced to the magnificent Elliot Gray, who now plays keys in the band. Their groovy drummer, Josh Schusterman, was a lucky find on craigslist to say the least!

Since the self-release of *Schizophonic*, Fortune Dwellers have been gigging regularly in the Seattle area. They are a group of fantastic musicians who can put on quite a show. Come see for yourself sometime!

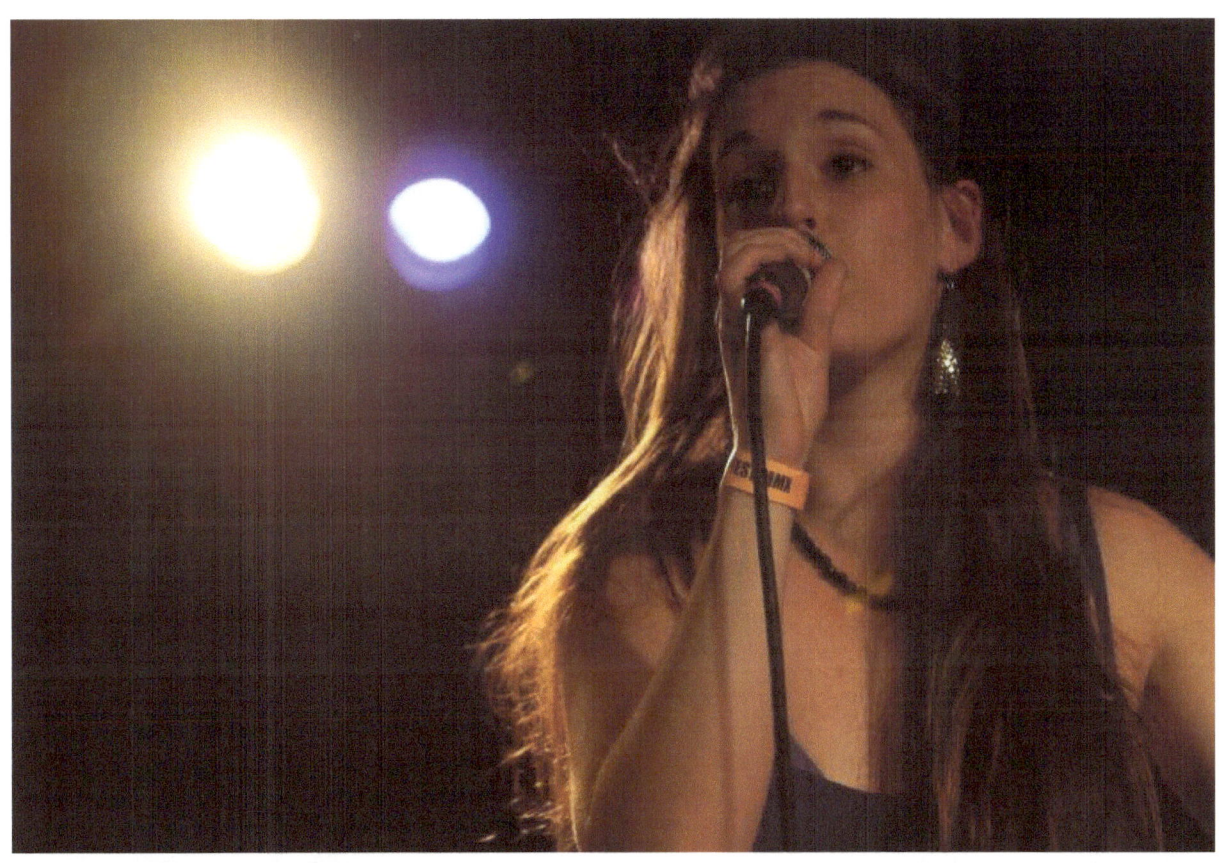

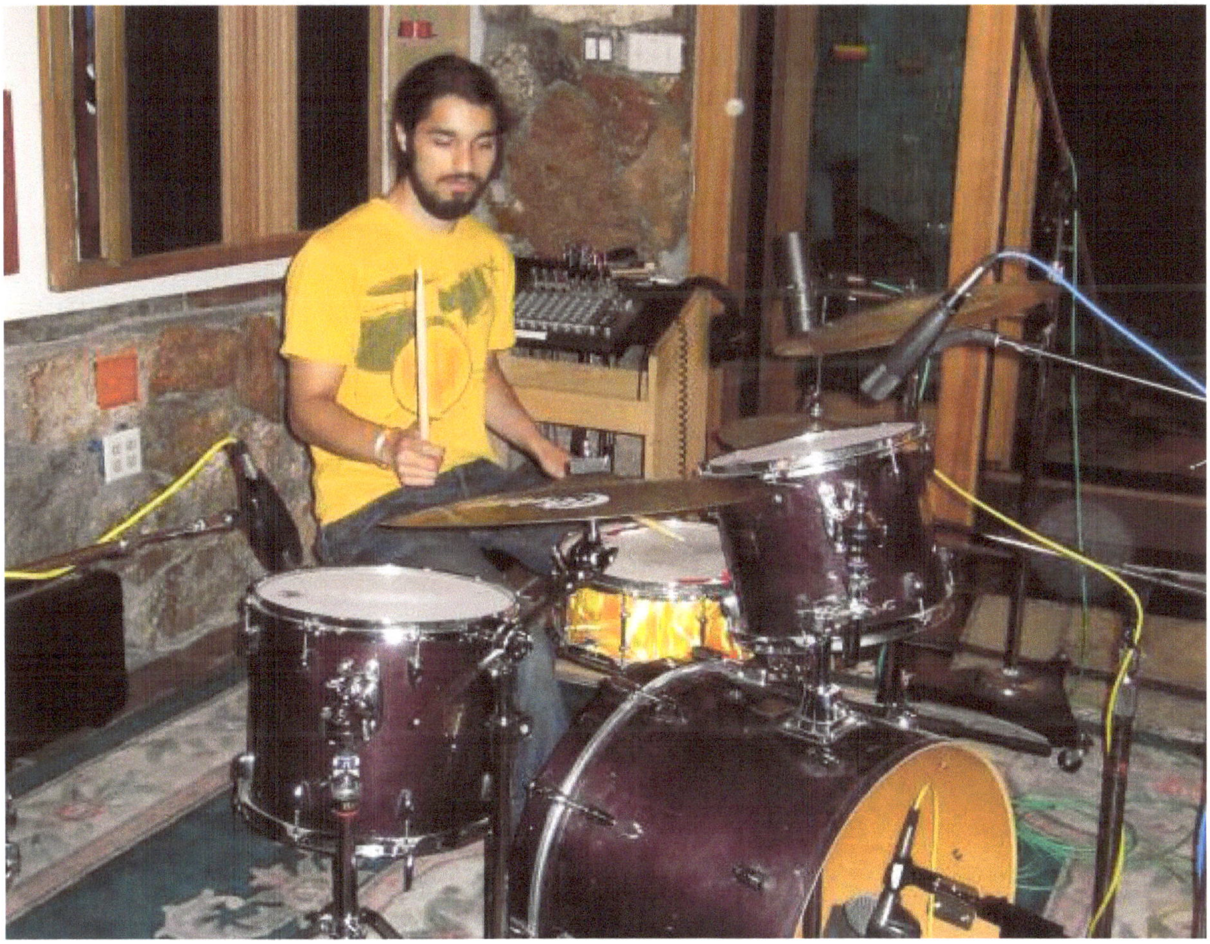

Fortune Dwellers

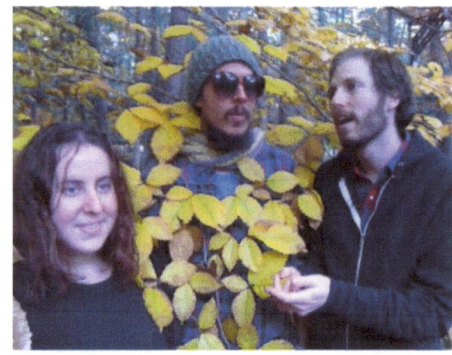 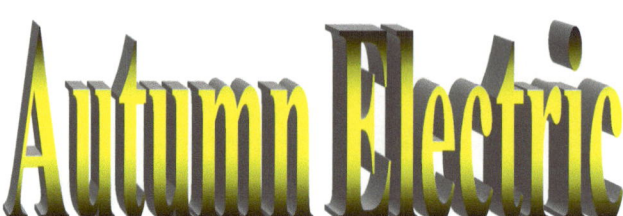

Autumn Electric formed loosely in fall of 2007. I snagged a few friends, namely: Jessica Eballar (banjo), Naomi Smith (Piano) and Gene Hardy (Bass), to play some live shows with me (Michael Trew). I'd played in a variety of grunge and progressive rock bands here in Seattle growing up. It was about this time I wanted to do something with more layers of pretty instrumentation and harmony. What led to some great early recordings, and being barely audible at loud bar concerts. By summer of 2008, we finished work on our debut record "Very Soon the Light" (at Jesse Tiamson's On the Air studio, Seattle WA), a sort of whispering, haunting ala Sufjan Stevens kind of thing. I recruited many friends to sing and play folksy instruments on it.

Naomi and I were in a previous band the Undercover Llamas with friend Micah Ellison. He had since been touring throughout U.S. and Europe with underground folk band June Madrona. One evening over dinner, he compelled us to go on tour... this led to a lot things. I decided to go on a backpacking trip through the UK in fall '08, followed immediately by a west coast tour. It was an epic 2 months of couch surfing, and song singing. I also realized touring was a great way to connect with friends and relatives in other states. Whereas traveling can be expensive, touring actually makes you money! if you're smart.

2009 was probably our most crazy year so far. Start with the addition of drummer Daniel Desrosiers, and replacement of Gene Hardy with bassist Kevin Gibbons. Dan and Kevin both grew up on the east coast. We quit working with our first manager, because I felt I knew better where the band should be playing etc. In the summer, we officially released "Very Soon the Light". This was a bittersweet celebration, due to it being a combination of a farewell show for banjo player Jessica Eballar. Gibbons quit the same night as a domino effect. We were in the middle of recording a new album, an effort based on new songs featuring the rhythm section, and works by Jessica. About that time, a friend Jeremiah Estes and I had become roommates and talked in length about how we needed to buy a van and road-trip the U.S. I purchased a huge Ford Econoline (Vandalf the Grey), much to the happiness of my girlfriend who was tired of driving us to gigs. At the time, Dan had been living on my couch for several months. Jeremy and I talked him into leaving his cat with a friend and going with us to the east coast. The trip soon turned into a tour, and 3 men soon turned into 3 men and 3 ladies (and a guinea pig).

The band was now Naomi, Dan and me. Naomi was filling in bass parts with her keyboards. We took some of the songs were had been recording, and added a couple more by way of On the Air studios, to create "We Breathe the Same Air". Jenifer (Naomi's close friend), my girlfriend Sarah (with Thomas the guinea pig), and Jeremiah rounded out our crew. We did a 6 week tour of the country, missing only 15 of the most central states. We had no label or management. Things were about to get crazy.

Life on the road is fun. Between the 6 of us, we had a relative or friend in almost every state. We drove down memory lanes of places we were born, forgot what day of the week it was all the time. We froze, while van-sleeping in Wyoming, overheated in Louisiana. We celebrated my 29th birthday, while driving through upstate New York, I turned around to see one of those 50cent apple pies with candles stuck in it. New Orleans was so much fun, I actually had to convince them to finish the rest of the tour! When we finally reached the west coast, our money situation got better and we did make back to Seattle alive.

At the moment we're enjoying working with a new 4th band mate, who strangely enough plays banjo among other things. Many new songs are in the works, with a theme of personal loss and cultural history of the NW. We've grown much more experimental and I feel something unique will come of it soon.

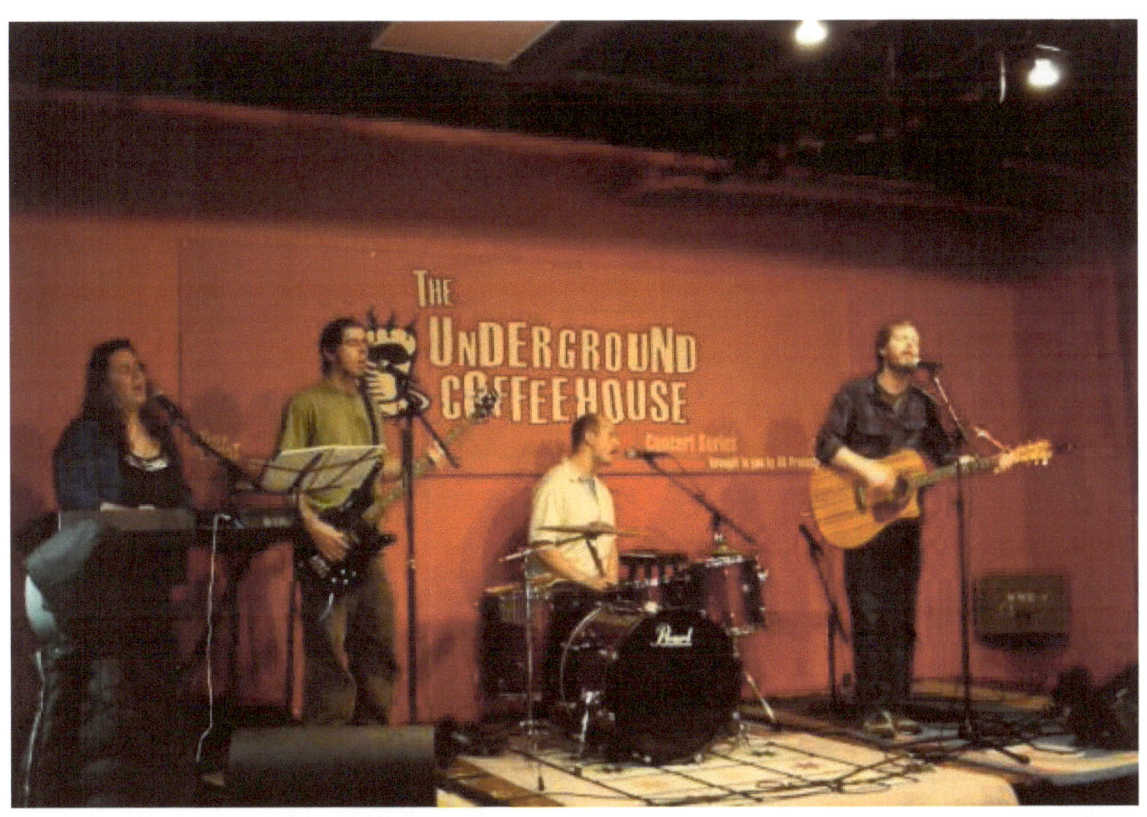

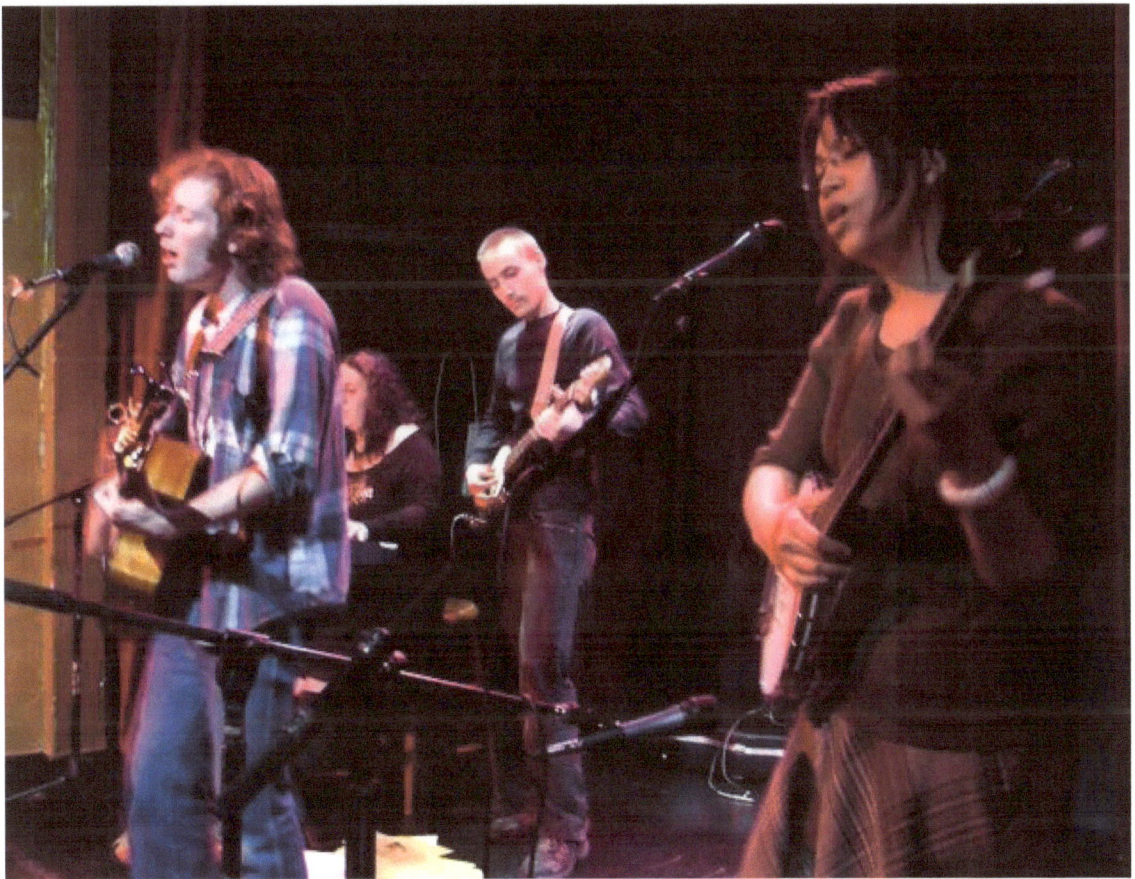

Autumn Electric

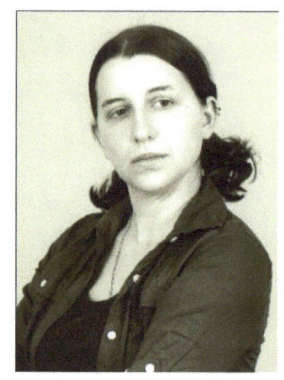

Susanne "Wolfgirl" Ranseen

I am a mostly self taught artist, and I have been perfecting my art since Junior High. My art is inspired the world around me, the images that dance through this thing in my head called an imagination, and the mythology/fairytales that I have read. My art style is all over the place from the realistic detail of my pointillism to the brush strokes of my impressionistic/abstract paintings. I find it works not to limit myself to one style or medium to work with.

When I first began getting serious about my artwork instead of just doodling odd creatures in the margins of my school books was in Junior High. In my seventh grade English class every student had to write a short 5 chapter story as our final. I got carried away writing several more chapters then that and adding illustrations to my story. Looking back at it now I cringe at both my art work and writing. In high school I was part of a painting group. Every Saturday I would bundle up my oil and acrylic paints and the random things I had sketched. My work was mostly fantasy that I desperately tried to make look realistic. I got frustrated that my art wasn't as "good" as the idea in my head or other painters in my group.

I learned my first real lesson about art then when my teacher, Jan, told me to not compare myself to others I had a gift for doing storybook images, I wasn't competing with the others to be the best just myself.

In college between working hard for my degree, friends, clubs, and work my art became a side note it wasn't responsible to draw a dragon when I had a big chemistry test coming up. I took an art class to complement my studies "Scientific Drawing" with Jim. Jim taught me how to look at something and see it in its parts so that I could put it onto a page. My heart leapt at the challenge of pointillism. Now the major form of art I do. My first pointillism was "Baby Mine" it took me over 36 hours and several weeks to complete. I drove my friends' nuts with the sound of the tapping pen. I had found the way to capture realism, something that had escaped my grasp for years in paint and pencil.

I have used my art as an escape, as a way to experience the world around me, and a way to connect to others. I take my pen and paper most anywhere with me. So I can work on a piece, such as my pointillism, or hurriedly sketch an idea for a painting or drawing. I tear things that catch my imagination out of magazines and write lines from books. My computer is full of my photograph of animals and people, any of which can turn into a fantastic dream or a realistic image. I am open to the next thing, the next experience, and the next emotion that will go into my art.

So I would say my last great lesson in art is to not close your mind and breathe in the second of your life in this world to create something that will last beyond you. May your spirit be feed and your works capture the minds and hearts of others.

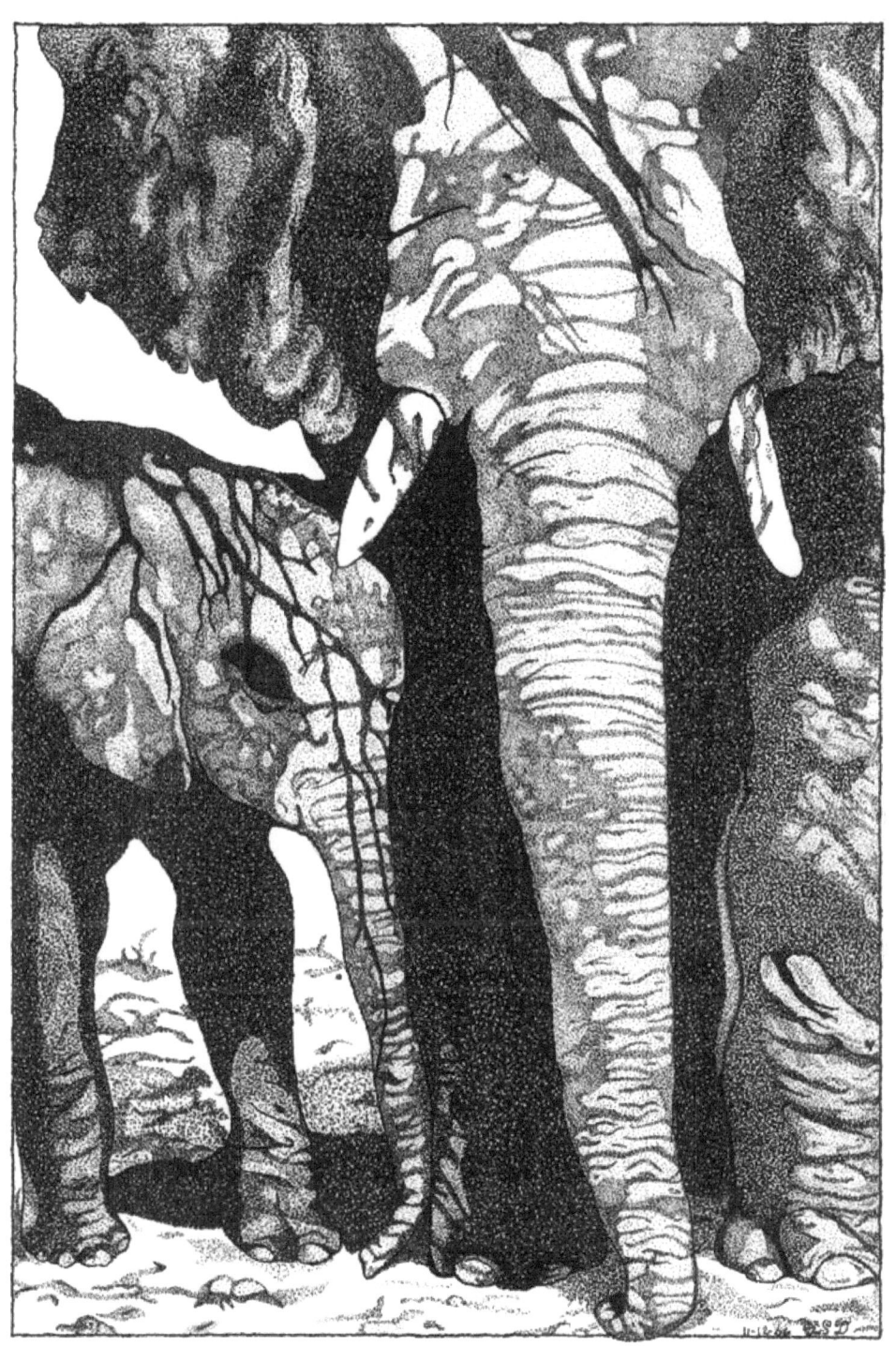

"Baby Mine" Susanne Ranseen, Micro pens on Bristol Paper, 2006

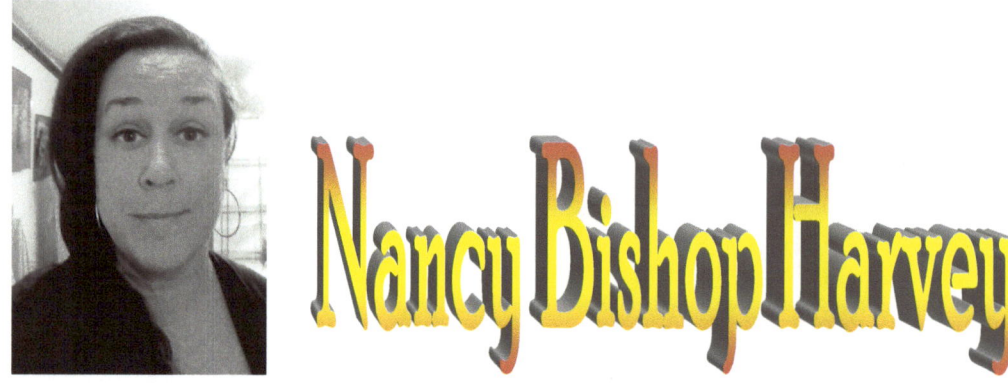

Nancy Bishop Harvey

I am an artist because that is an area that I have finally found my niche, or at least I think I have. When I am out in the studio, I can get lost in enthusiasm, passion, and creativity. It is an outlet for good and bad thoughts, feelings of inadequacy or euphoria, and a tool for self preservation and betterment. It is where I want to be, where I feel I can do the best I can and possibly make a difference, where the 'where' isn't relevant anymore.

It is a constant struggle to achieve the 'artist' label in the opinion of others, or what they understand *to be* an artist. Therefore, while at times it is extremely satisfying, emotionally and intellectually stimulating, it can be a giant void of disappointment that can lead to periods of no art being created at all, which can be dangerous for the psyche and soul. Yet, when I do become involved in the creative process, all slips away, and the mind begins to really think, ponder, analyze, and invent. It is a great thing to be an artist - to have the clear 'canvas' to lay the foundation of what is to come, that which may not have been thought of as yet, but will undoubtedly become clearer with every stroke of the brush or pen.

I think that art is the avenue I can screen my ideas, laying new ones in the process, and utilizing everything around me to develop a better self within. You know, I think everyone is an artist in one way or another. I was told once by a professor that I deeply admired that you have to choose whether you create art for 'art's sake' or for commercial purposes…..it seems I have chosen the first, and I am not sure that we can't do both…but everyone has to look within themselves, and decide *why* they are creating.

Always be true to yourself, and BE YOURSELF…it will be hard when you see the falseness around you, especially at the art openings, but fly high, and you will get there eventually, probably much sooner than I. I still have faith that I will get somewhere someday…this can carry us for a long time. Let the artist in you spring into action, and do not be discouraged. The sky is the limit!!

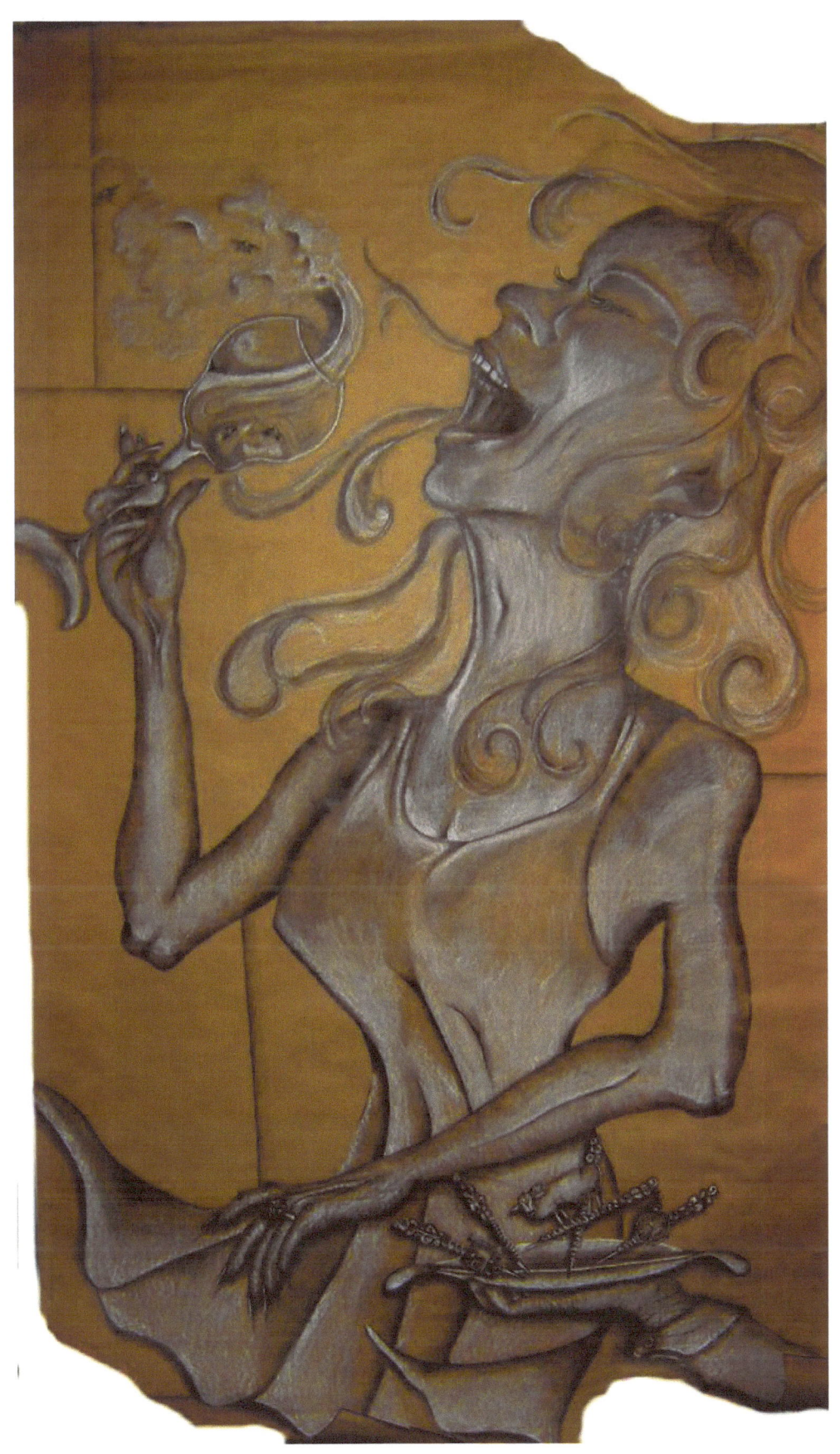

"Denail" Nancy Bishop, ebony pencil, green acrylic highlights, white conte on brown paper...4' w x 7' h, 2001

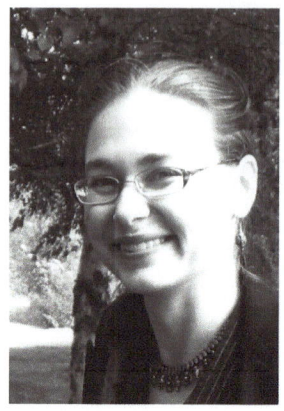 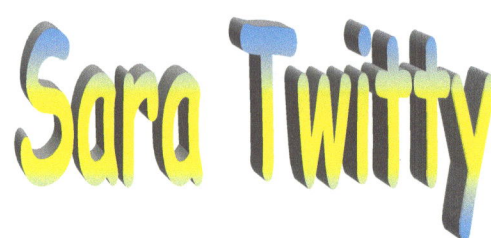

The first time I seriously considered being an artist was in community college. I had, like many others, been drawing since I was young, but I was hardly a virtuoso. As a kid I used to take tracing paper and copy out the figures from my comic books. I doodled fuzzy monsters on my homework along with algebra and felt positively inspired when it occurred to me I could add light and shadow to a character. I never thought about trying to make a career of it though, until I sat in my first proper art class and heard my teacher, a wonderful and inspiring man, talk about how he knew he was destined to be an artist back in kindergarten because he had the only stick figure with bubble feet. I laughed and laughed, and thought, huh, that could be me.

I realized that I enjoyed art more then anything else in school, and also that it was not about talent, but desire. I liked doing art. I was always thinking about it, drawing scenes from stories, and drooling over picture books by Froud, Pyle, and Rackham. So I went to Art Center College of Design in Pasadena, California and through practice I began to gain some skill.

I learned what the purpose behind all those mystical pots and tools in the art stores were. Paint became a medium to enjoy and play with, rather then fear because it didn't erase, and my figures began to look more like people and less like distorted putty. I discovered a new love of landscapes and backgrounds and happily pursued a major in entertainment art. Dreamily picturing the day I might get to walk into a bookstore and see my own art on the cover of a novel.

To me art, especially illustration is about communication. It's like the old saying "A picture is worth a thousand words." In a very literal way, it could take a thousand words to describe in prose the exact color, and light and content of a painting. Having had to write several essays giving minute descriptions of famous works, and I can tell you those thousand words get eaten up quickly.

To an extent I can judge how well I execute a painting by what people see when they look at it, and how much of what I intended to say is readable. Did a painting that I meant to be funny come off as such, or do people see something else. At the same time, there is an unexpected collaboration between artist and viewer when someone sees your work that I find fascinating. People are an amalgam of history, experience and associations that I could never predict in my wildest dreams.

Sometimes they see things I never thought about, much less intended. They read a different story from the image, yet if I cock my head and squint I can see it there too. All interpretations are valid because they are all real, and I think that is what I find most moving about art. From the greatest fine art of the day, to the kitschiest greeting card, it all has something in it for someone.

I like to focus my personal art on imaginary subjects that are whimsical or exaggerated. I enjoy the freedom I can find in stylizing and bringing together disparate elements, and letting emotion rather then practicality drive subject matter. Art is a great venue for expression, and for me many emotional things come to me first as imagery. Putting that onto paper and getting it out is a way to reveal, and sometimes confront myself. Painting can be a mellowing activity, for me, almost Zen. I reach a state of concentration where I am thinking only about brush and paint, and everything else is temporarily forgotten. I must be careful to never leave a pot on the stove.

I work mostly in digital painting, on Photoshop or Corel Painter, and dabble with acrylic and watercolor. When I can I like to sit in museums and sketch from famous portraits, or photographs, or just out of my own head. At the moment I am trying to establish myself as an illustrator in Seattle. I'm pursuing freelance contract work, looking for positions at gaming and entertainment studios, and working on personal art pieces for myself, competitions, and a creative literary journal started by a friend.

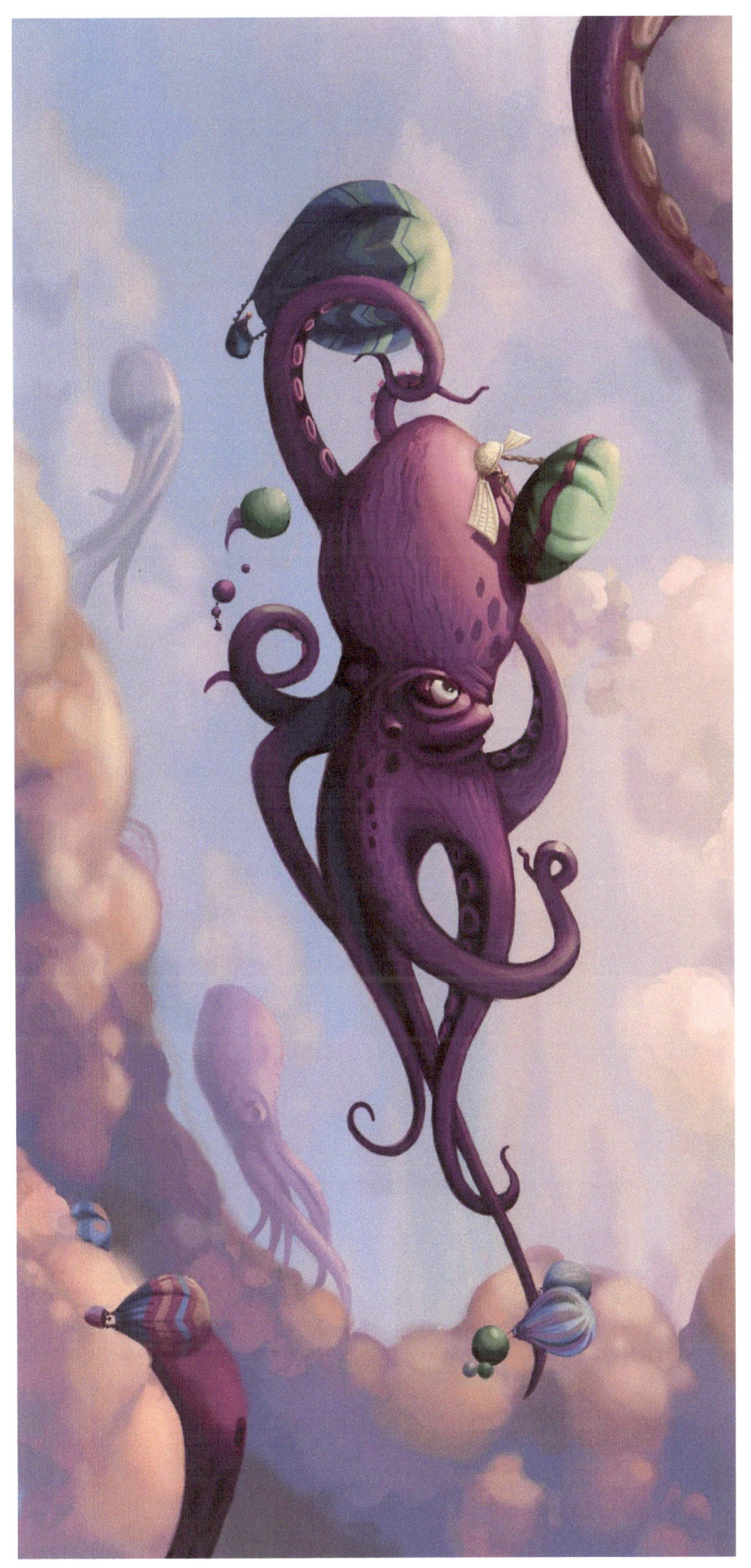

"Octopus" Sara Twitty

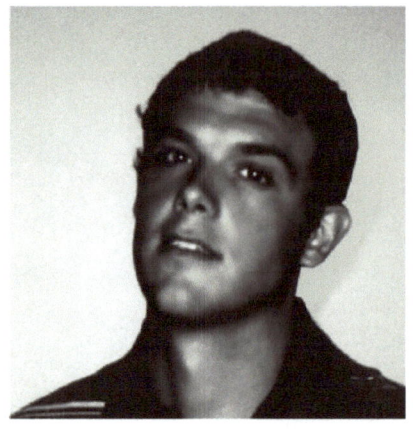

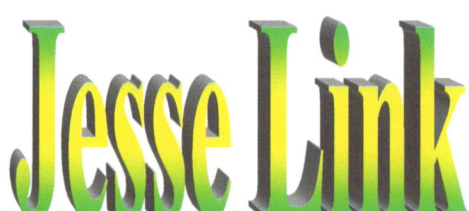

I'm inspired by urban culture, the immense wilderness of the Pacific Northwest and the contradiction between the two. Seattle is a perfect example of that contradiction. It's a bustling urban city completely surrounded by the incredible wilderness. It has to be one of the few cities in the United States were you can see bald eagles on your morning bike ride to the coffee shop. It's the balance of two completely contradictory forces that I seek to achieve in my work. Urban is my style of painting with use of aerosols, stencils, textile prints and a bold color palette combined to create beautiful images of animals and a spirit of nature.

Seattle is my inspiration while my goal is to excite the viewer and stimulate curiosity and thought. At one moment you can be walking down a busy city street feeling completely urban. Then, between two buildings, catch a view of snowcapped mountains, rolling hills and icy water. Instantly your feelings change as you pay attention to that deep connection we all have with nature. I think experiencing that contradiction can be very stimulating.

It's that experience I want to recreate by combining imagery from nature, urban style, physical distress/organic decay and manmade elements such as ideas, letters or numbers. All of these elements are then carefully organized to imply an intentionally open ended narrative. For each of us our perceptions are our reality. The same is true for the narrative. It's meaning is dependent on the perceptions of the viewer. To define the narrative is to look within yourself and having the viewer look within themselves to create meaning is what I hope to achieve.

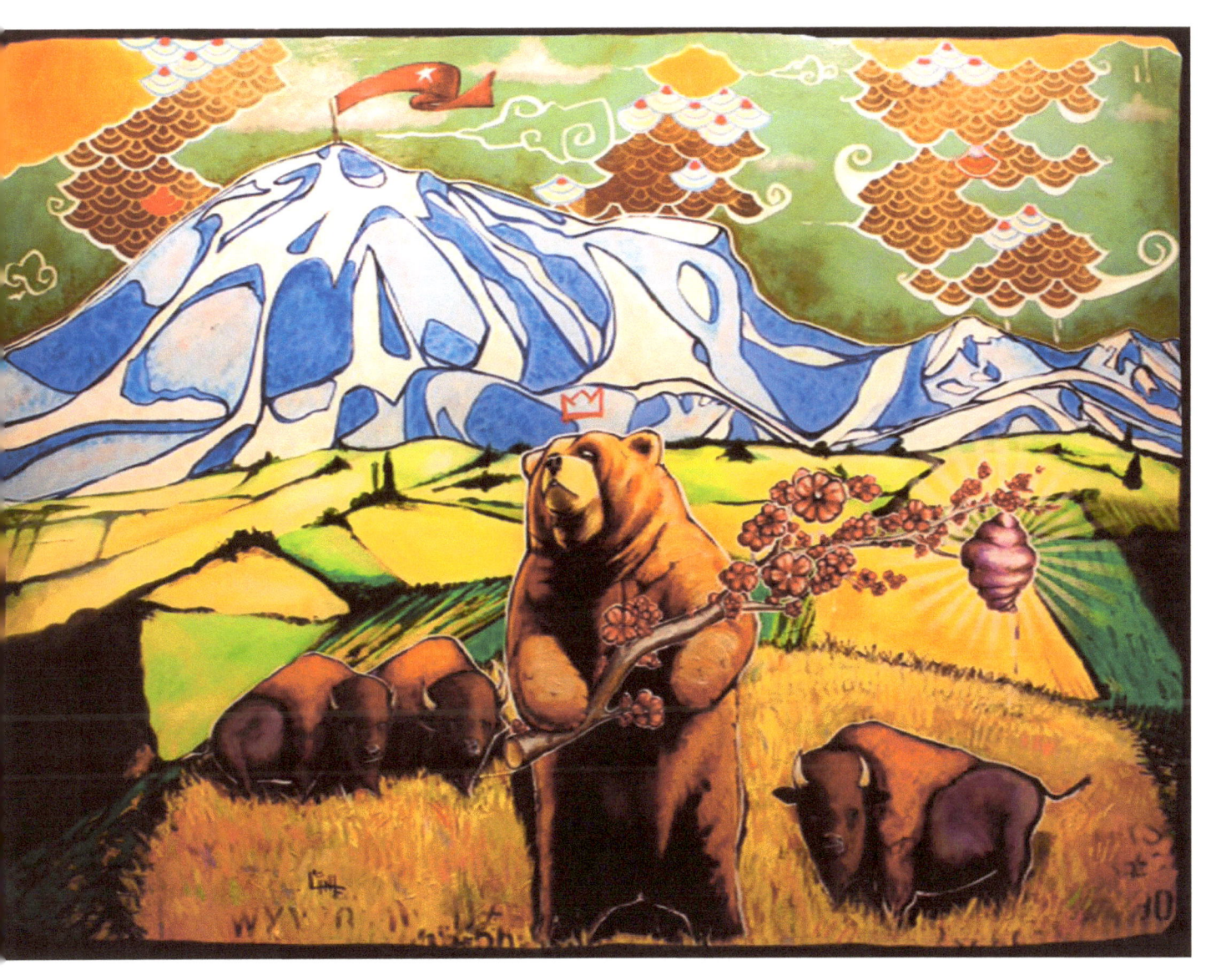

"Origins of Self- Reliance" Jesse Link

Ending Note

Every artist has their own style, their own opinions, and their own voice. There are those who will try to hide from it all, but let it be seen and let be heard. –Sarah Ghanooni

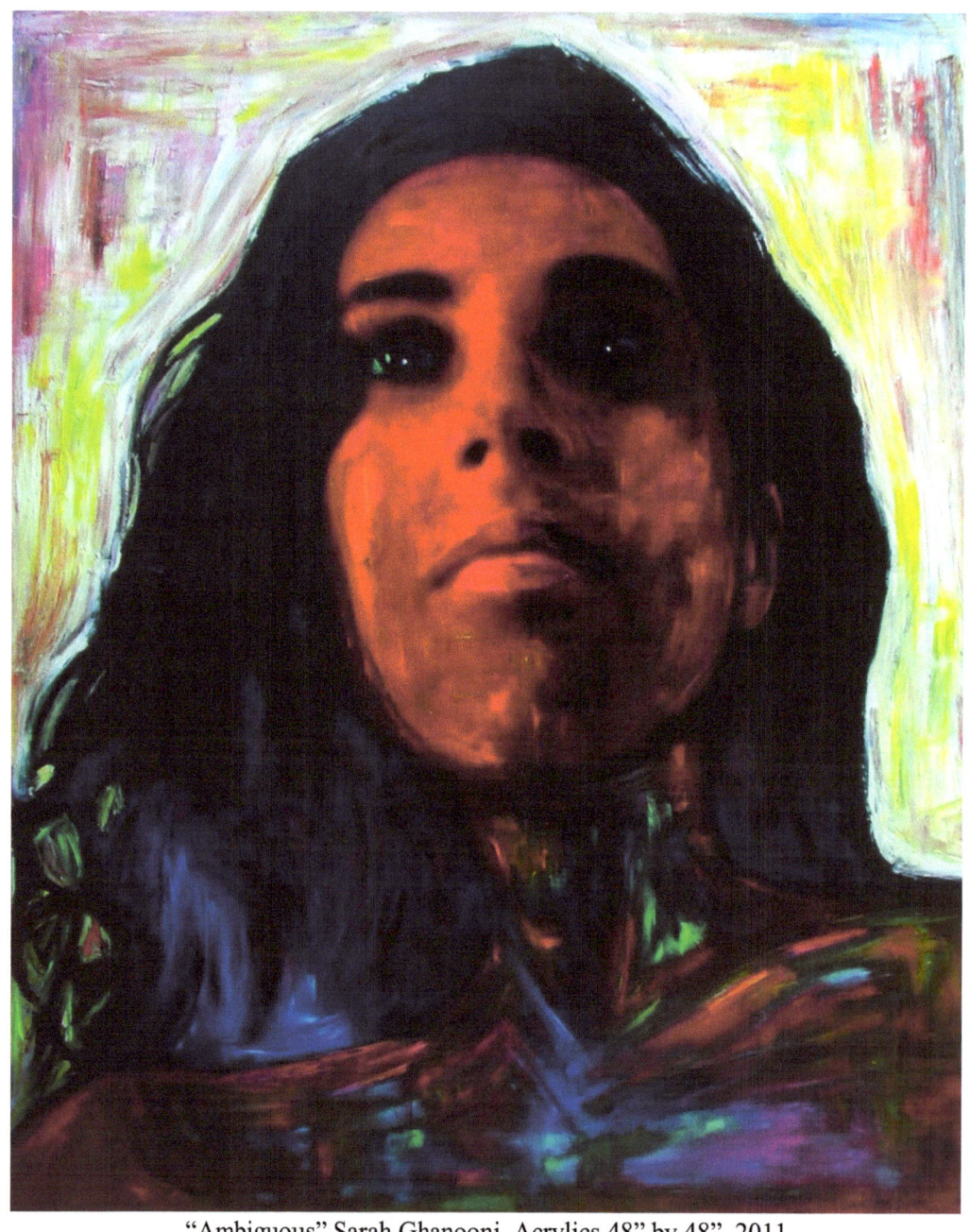

"Ambiguous" Sarah Ghanooni, Acrylics 48" by 48", 2011

www.ingramcontent.com/pod-product-compliance
Lightning Source LLC
Chambersburg PA
CBHW050741180526
45159CB00003B/1312